THE
GLORIOUS
WORLD CUP

THE GLORIOUS WORLD CUP

A Fanatic's Guide

Alan Black
and
David Henry Sterry

NEW AMERICAN LIBRARY

New American Library
Published by New American Library, a division of
Penguin Group (USA) Inc., 375 Hudson Street,
New York, New York 10014, USA
Penguin Group (Canada), 90 Eglinton Avenue East, Suite 700, Toronto,
Ontario M4P 2Y3, Canada (a division of Pearson Penguin Canada Inc.)
Penguin Books Ltd., 80 Strand, London WC2R 0RL, England
Penguin Ireland, 25 St. Stephen's Green, Dublin 2,
Ireland (a division of Penguin Books Ltd.)
Penguin Group (Australia), 250 Camberwell Road, Camberwell, Victoria 3124,
Australia (a division of Pearson Australia Group Pty. Ltd.)
Penguin Books India Pvt. Ltd., 11 Community Centre, Panchsheel Park,
New Delhi - 110 017, India
Penguin Group (NZ), 67 Apollo Drive, Rosedale, North Shore 0632,
New Zealand (a division of Pearson New Zealand Ltd.)
Penguin Books (South Africa) (Pty.) Ltd., 24 Sturdee Avenue,
Rosebank, Johannesburg 2196, South Africa

Penguin Books Ltd., Registered Offices:
80 Strand, London WC2R 0RL, England

First published by New American Library,
a division of Penguin Group (USA) Inc.

First Printing, May 2010
10 9 8 7 6 5 4 3 2 1

Copyright © Alan Black and David Sterry, 2010
All rights reserved

See page 136 for cover photo credits and permissions.

REGISTERED TRADEMARK—MARCA REGISTRADA

Set in Garamond
Designed by Kim Sillen Gledhill

Printed in the United States of America

PUBLISHER'S NOTE
While the author has made every effort to provide accurate telephone numbers and Internet
addresses at the time of publication, neither the publisher nor the author assumes any responsibility
for errors, or for changes that occur after publication. Further, publisher does not have any control
over and does not assume any responsibility for author or third-party Web sites or their content.

The Glorious World Cup

LET THERE BE MADNESS AGAIN

It's all about the glory. Hundreds of millions of people gathering in squares, parks, bars, barns, caves and bunkers, some crossing deserts just to find a radio that's broadcasting a match. It's humanity's biggest pilgrimage. It's the World Cup Finals. This book is a celebration of the passion, the madness, the insanity, the joy, the sorrow, the pity, the tragedy and the glory of being alive, of being human, of giving yourself over body and soul to the beautiful game. And how it's all coming home to roost in the cradle of civilization: Africa.

Winter 2010, South Africa — the planet is going mad. Over a billion people will be perched on the edges of their seats, watching the biggest show on earth. Forget the Olympics and the Super Bowl; soccer is king when it comes to fans and viewers. And in America, tens of millions who play and follow soccer are hoping, praying, dreaming that this is the year when Team USA finally puts it all together on the biggest stage there is, and shows the world that we are, at long last, Players. We want our goalie Tim Howard to be added to the golden list that includes England's Gordon Banks, and Italy's Dino Zoff. We want Clint Dempsey to join the ranks of Zinedine Zidane of France, Brazil's Ronaldo, and Germany's Gerd Müller in the pantheon of goal-scoring gods. We want Bob Bradley to be mentioned in the same breath as Sir Alf Ramsey of England, Germany's Franz Beckenbauer, and Brazil's Mario Zagallo when talking about brilliant World Cup winning tacticians. This is part of the beauty of it. Soccer allows us to dream huge, and hope to spring eternal.

1

THE DRAW
FOR THE
2010 WORLD CUP FINALS

Group A: South Africa, Mexico, Uruguay, France

Group B: Argentina, South Korea, Nigeria, Greece

Group C: England, (USA) Algeria, Slovenia

Group D: Germany, Australia, Ghana, Serbia

Group E: Netherlands, Japan, Cameroon, Denmark

Group F: Italy, New Zealand, Paraguay, Slovakia

Group G: Brazil, North Korea, Ivory Coast, Portugal

Group H: Spain, Honduras, Chile, Switzerland

• The top two teams in each group progress to the Round of 16.

• The Round of 16 takes place June 26–29 with the Quarterfinals on July 2 and 3.

• The Semifinals will be played in Cape Town on July 6, and in Durban on July 7.

• The World Cup Final will be staged in Johannesburg on Sunday, July 11.

The Finals kick off on June 11 in Johannesburg when hosts South Africa meet Mexico. The United States open their campaign with a huge game against England on June 12 in Rustenburg, sixty years after they defeated England 1-0 in the1950 World Cup Finals, followed by matches against Slovenia on June 18 in Johannesburg, and their final game in Group C against Algeria in Pretoria, on June 23.

The draw has thrown up some exciting clashes. Germany faces tough competition from the technically excellent Serbia and the gutsy Australians. Brazil is in the Group of Death, the tournament's toughest group, and comes up against a defensive North Korea appearing in the Finals after a forty-four-year absence. Tough games against Portugal and Ivory Coast will test the mettle of the five-time world champions. Heavily fancied Spain meets Chile in Group H. The Chileans played some of the best attacking soccer in the qualification process. In Group F, Italy will have to be on guard against rank outsiders New Zealand, keen to shock the world champions, while Diego Maradona's Argentina will have to step up their game in a tricky group to qualify for the Round of 16.

Welcome to SOUTH AFRICA

The history of South Africa can be found on hundreds of soccer fields, from Cape Town to Soweto to Johannesburg; from manicured lawns of the rich and famous, to glass-strewn inner-city asphalt jungles, to the mighty jungle where the lion sleeps tonight. Soccer is, has been, and always will be the game of the people, in part because all you need is one ball, twenty-two able-bodied souls, and a heart full of dreams.

When the smoke of apartheid cleared, and the dust settled, soccer then became a way of healing the hate of a nation so violently torn apart. In 1992, after decades of South Africa being excluded from international competitions because of boycotts, an ebony and ivory national team, Bafana Bafana (Zulu for "The Boys") competed for the first time. They defeated Cameroon on the strength of a penalty kick by Doctor Khumalo. Then in 1996, Bafana Bafana showed South Africa just what could happen when black and white worked together in perfect harmony. They won the Africa Cup. The nation rejoiced, embraced the change, and reveled in the game of the people. World Cup 2010 is a celebration of a decade of democracy, as the international balls-out glory of soccer reigns in this new land of freedom.

SOUTH AFRICA: THE LAY OF THE LAND

South Africa is about the size of the West Coast of America, scrunched together like a potato, instead of stretched out like a banana. Since it is at the very tip of
the continent, the southern edge of the country is a coastline. On one side: camels, drought and desert, and on the other side: lions, tigers and jungle. Throw in some massive mountains, the world's biggest meteor crater, semi-Arctic winter locales and some of the hottest spots on Earth, and there you have it: South Africa.

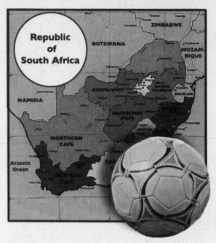

SOUTH AFRICA — HISTORY AS SOCCER

South Africa is the Cradle of Humankind. A four-million-year-old human skeleton was discovered in 1996. He was called Little Foot, chiefly because he could strike a soccer ball so fiercely with either of his tiny feet. A legendary dribbler, early cave drawings show him scoring a hat trick against an international rival in an early version of the World Cup, 3,998,999 years ago. Sadly, his career was cut short by a broken bone, the results of a barbaric tackle by a local hard man, Big Foot.

Soccer-playing tribes developed all over South Africa, among them Shangaan, Tswana, Zulus, and the Hottentots, some of whom broke off to become Tottenham Hotspur in the English soccer league. About a thousand years ago, a great civilization developed, aided by player-transfer trades with Asia and Europe. In 1298, it culminated in the competition for the Lost City of Gold Cup, with the winners presented with Mapungubwe's famed gold foil rhinoceros, and the losers executed.

In 1652, Dutch commander Jan van Riebeeck was sent by the

Dutch East India Company to build a fort, develop a vegetable garden, and look for soccer players, specifically reliable goal scorers, hard-nosed central defenders, and sure-handed goalkeepers. At first, trading of soccer knowledge and players was extremely amicable. But in 1795, the English, hungry to exploit the rich vein of soccer talent, stormed in and crippled the Dutch with vicious knee-breaking tackles, and sent them packing.

Gradually, the Europeans formed their own nation, and they called themselves Afrikaners, or Boers. Two of their descendants, in fact, played for the Dutch national team—Frank and Ronald de Boer. However, the Zulus, under chieftains Shaka and King Cetshwayo, both soccer nuts, would not back down, and they led several brilliant teams to great victories including a resounding thumping of the British at Isandhlwana in 1879.

For many years afterward, blacks and whites were not allowed to play together, and soccer suffered. Certainly there were many people responsible for the death of apartheid. But first on that list has to be soccer fanatic Nelson Mandela. Imprisoned because he demanded equal rights for all people, he was unable to attend any soccer matches for twenty-seven years. But when he got out, he made up for lost time. He was able to unite all races, colors, and creeds through the game, and the national team. And when Bafana Bafana won the

Africa Cup in 1996, Nelson Mandela danced on the field afterward.

Which brings us to 2010. It took centuries of suffering, sacrifice, and selflessness to bring the World Cup to a country that was banned from all international sports for decades. But finally the epicenter of the soccer universe will come to roost in the new symbol for unity and equality: South Africa.

VUVUZELA

That sound you hear, like a billion bees buzzing, is South Africa loving her soccer. It's the sound of a vuvuzela. According to African legend, "a baboon is killed by big noise." And that's what the crazed fans are trying to do. Kill off their opponents with a big, big noise. Or is that just post-Afrikaner propaganda propagated by the makers of the vuvuzela? According to some, there is no connection between the vuvuzela and the trumpets made in Africa from kudu horns in days of yore. According to some, it's just a cheap fabricated excuse to inflict permanent damage on the eardrums, while making for the manufacturers big, big coin.

During the 2009 Confederations Cup in South Africa, many European white men were incensed by the sound. Players from Spain and pundits from England, all called for a ban on the vuvuzela during the 2010 Finals. But commentators around the world, as well as the powers-that-be in World Cup soccer, stepped in quickly, and spoke from on high.

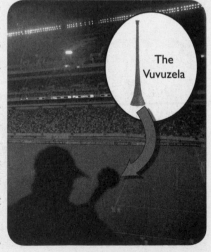

The
Vuvuzela

"This is what African and South African football is all about: noise, excitement, dancing, shouting and enjoyment...Let us embrace the vuvuzela and whatever else the South African World Cup throws at us," said the BBC's Farayi Mungazi. He was echoed by Sepp Blatter, president of FIFA. "We should not try to Europeanize an African World Cup."

Whether you like it or not, it looks like the big noise of the vuvuzela will be the defining sound of World Cup 2010 in South Africa. The whole world is waiting to see exactly which baboons die.

VENUES

Cape Town, Green Point Stadium, Capacity: 70,000

At the tip of the African continent, Table Mountain looms high over the Mother City, and served as a flat top landmark for centuries of travelers. Cape Town has a world-class melting pot feel, as cultures of many ilk rub elbows. It represents the best and the worst in South Africa: surrounded by spectacular physical beauty, but home to Robben Island, an infamous black hole that became a world-famous symbol for evil when Nelson Mandela was jailed there.

Durban, King Senzangakhona Stadium, Capacity: 70,000

The Golden Mile is a perfect name for a stop on the road to the World Cup. And it is that magical stretch of sun- soaked subtropical beaches, world-class dining emporiums, and crazy-colored rickshaws bustling through promenades that define Durban, the busiest port

in all of Africa. Surrounded by spectacular dunes, reefs, reed-filled wetlands and huge blue mountains, it is a place where you can satisfy all your shopping and sunbathing needs in one fell swoop.

Johannesburg, Ellis Park Stadium, Capacity: 60,000; Soccer City Stadium, Capacity: 94,700

Jozi, Joni, or Joburg, as Johannesburg is known to the locals, is the biggest city in South Africa. It is the beating economic heart of sub-Saharan Africa. Diamonds, gold, and a spectacular world-class skyline define this City of Lights. Giant skyscrapers house multinational corporations, awe-inspiring restaurants, and jaw-dropping shopping opportunities, from high-end boutiques to street vendors who peddle their wares to those searching for bargains galore.

Ellis Park was one of the first modern stadiums in South Africa and has housed soccer and rugby slugfests for decades. Soccer City Stadium, on the other hand, is not just a soccer venue. It has hosted history itself. When it came time to hold a rally for Nelson Mandela, when he was finally released from prison, Soccer City was the spot. And now, as the world looks to South Africa to get its World Cup fix, all eyes will be on Soccer City in Jozi—the venue for the World Cup Final.

Mangaung/Bloemfontein, Free State Stadium, Capacity: 45,000

Mangaung means "Place of the Cheetahs" in Sesotho. Bloemfontein means "flower fountain" in Dutch. And that, as much as anything, defines this urban but rural, sandstone-rich, landlocked capital of the Free State Province. It is known far and wide as the City of Roses. From a thrill-filled ride at the Bloemfontein Kart Club, to a sleepover at the zoo, to a trip to Boyden Observatory, Mangaung/Bloemfontein is a feast for the eyes as well as the nose.

Nelson Mandela Bay/Port Elizabeth,
The Nelson Mandela Stadium, Capacity: 48,000

Spectacular beaches, an opera house, an absolutely fabulous collection of Victorian and Art Nouveau buildings, and the home of Nelson Mandela as well as many of the other figures in the struggle against apartheid. And in the distance looms Hogsback, rumored to be Tolkien's inspiration for parts of the *Lord of the Rings* books.

Nelspruit Mpumalanga,
Mbombela Stadium, Capacity: 46,000

"Place where the sun rises." That's what Nelspruit Mpumalanga means in SiSwati. God's Window looks out over rivers of blue and fields of green, the whole thing with a distinct feel like a Garden of Eden; mangoes and macadamia nuts, wild waterfalls and wild horses, giraffes and bushbucks, hippos and rhinos, with ivory poachers lurking. World-famous Kruger National Park is just a hop, skip, and a jump away.

Polokwane, Peter Mokaba Stadium, Capacity: 45,000

Polokwane means "place of safety." And it is one of the most famous destinations for big-game hunters. Coincidence? Certainly not. Home to some of the most amazing wildlife on the planet, it has become a happening destination for ecotourists from all over the world. The Peter Mokaba Stadium was named after Peter Mokaba, a leader in the African National Congress Youth League.

Rustenburg, The Royal Bafokeng Stadium, Capacity: 45,000

Rustenburg nestles like a throbbing knob in the fertile foothills of the take-your-breath-away Magaliesburg Mountains. Gorgeous as it is to look at, it is even richer in natural resources. First the fertile soil gave locals and Afrikaners fruits and nuts, tobacco and corn, but what was discovered underneath the dirt changed this place forever. Platinum. Just down the road is Sun City, home of world-class sporting events for many decades.

Tshwane/Pretoria, Loftus Versfeld Stadium, Capacity: 51,762

Tshwane/Pretoria is the home of the South African mint, which just keeps pumping out rands. It is one of the country's trifecta of capital cities. With architecture that reflects English Colonialism, Art Deco and homegrown South African styles, as well as the National Zoological Gardens of South Africa, it is a city steeped in tradition, yet burning with modernism, a unique blend of bustling urban life and spectacular natural beauty.

photos
by Stefan Meisel

Steven Pienaar

illustration by Liu Yuhua

BORN:
March 17,1982
Westbury,
Johannesburg,
South Africa

HEIGHT: 5'9"

POSITION:
Midfielder

NICKNAME: Schillo for short (after Salvatore Schillaci)

QUOTE: "A happy team is a winning team and that is what we are aiming to be."

CELEBRATION: Double somersault

PERSONAL SONG CHANTED BY FANS:
"I am the Music Man, I come from far away, and I can play (what can you play?)
I Play The Pienaar! Pi Pi Pienaaaaaar!"

From lookout boy for drug dealers, to the School of Excellence, to winning a Dutch championship with Ajax, to a proud member of Bafana Bafana by the time he was twenty-one. This was the career trajectory for Steven Pienaar. And how did he go from juvenile delinquent to playing in the World Cup 2002 in Korea/Japan? Dogged hard work, shocking physical skill, and brilliant control. He has the eye of the tiger, and the heart of the lion.

German giants Borussia Dortmund called, and Pienaar answered, leaving his beloved Ajax team behind. That was when it all went terribly wrong. He couldn't find his German legs. His teammates gave him the coldest of shoulders. It escalated into an ugly confrontation in the dressing room. *I'm not welcome here, so I want to go.* That was what Steven told his boss. But instead of sulking and moaning, he decided to focus on soccer and his charity work, which specializes in helping teenagers who are in trouble in South Africa.

Like a knight in shining armor, Everton came to the rescue, and Pienaar became an instant hit, helping them reach the final of the English FA Cup. Even so, controversy managed to follow. When Pienaar scored a goal he lifted his shirt, revealing a message about his faith. The Football Association made it clear to Steven and Everton that such displays would not be tolerated. So when he scored again, he changed the celebration into a double somersault. South Africans, from Nelson Mandela to an army of soccer-mad kids, are hoping they see Steven Pienaar do double somersaults all over South Africa in 2010.

After receiving a warning about his flashing of religious messages, Pienaar changed the celebratory moves to a double somersault.

UNDERDOGS:
ALGERIA

Spain '82
El Molinón Stadium, Gijón

Infiesto is a small village in Asturias in Spain. The Algerian national team settled there for their stay during the 1982 Finals. No one paid much attention to them. Another small team destined to be flattened by the tournament's heavyweights. West Germany prepared the steamroller.

June 16, and hot, the stadium in Gijón was bursting with Algerians decked out in their national color of green. West Germany waltzed on to the field, certain they would dance Algeria off the cliff. But the soccer god was not listening to German Oom-pah. The Algerian Raï was about to make West Germany dance to a very different drummer.

The Africans opened the scoring. Germany's leader, Rummenigge, drew his team level. Drunken drafts of relief could be heard as far away as the Rhine. It lasted forty seconds. From the restart, Algeria stormed up field, and scored a goal of immeasurable quality. The Germans were stunned. The stadium erupted, the Algerian nation went berserk, and millions of underdogs everywhere cheered the demise of the steamroller.

Later, reports from Infiesto told of a huge party in the town. Asturians and Africans united in the joy of underdog victory. The Desert Warriors of Algeria catapulted themselves into World Cup history. The foundation for the rise of African soccer had been laid.

IRVINE WELSH

I remember my dad was lying in his bed, really hungover, probably still drunk, and he was euphoric. I was just a wee guy at the time. I thought Scotland had won the World Cup because they had beaten England. When I found out I was wrong, I couldn't get my head around it. I felt cheated, and I've felt that way ever since.

The first World Cup I was aware of was England '66. I was just getting into football. It was a few months the actual tournament, when Scotland played world champions England, at Wembley. My old man was going down for the game. He had family living in London. I was really excited that he was going, and I remember him returning home. Scotland had won. The victory was famous. We beat the World Cup winners. We beat the English.

The first World Cup I really got into was the 1970 World Cup with the fantastic Brazil team and its famous five of Pelé, Jairzinho, Rivelino, Tostão and Carlos Alberto. My team, Hibernian FC, had toured Brazil in the 1950s, when Hibs (Hibernian) were known for their own famous five: Ormond, Turnbull, Reilly, Johnstone and Smith. They played a game against Vasco de Gama in Rio in this incredible heat, and after twenty minutes, Hibs were up three-nil. The game finished 3-3 as the Hibs boys melted.

The Brazilian newspapers were amazed at Hibs style of play, an interchanging passing game that was unknown in Brazil. Brazilian legends like Garrincha and the top Brazilian coaches were impressed, and soon enough Brazilian football had adopted the Hibs style of play. And that explains why Brazil won the World Cup in 1970. They copied Hibs.

In the mid-to-late seventies, I was most enthusiastic about the Scottish football team. I went to games at Hampden when I could—it's what I did. I loved Hibs and my country but after the World Cup in Argentina in 1978, I lost interest. I remember when Scotland went to Argentina, and Ally MacLeod, the manager, whipped up the whole country into hysteria. Just before the Finals, we played England in Glasgow and lost 1-0 and I got this feeling that something was going to go fucking horribly wrong. I didn't believe the hype. MacLeod dismissed the result against the English as "the worst team won," but I knew then that he was cracking up under

the strain of the hype he had created. He said Scotland was going to win a medal. It ended in failure.

When Gemmill scored his famous goal for Scotland in Argentina in 1978, against Holland, I was on the edge of my seat watching it with my old man. Here was this wee Scottish guy dribbling his way through a large Dutch wall on his way to one of the great goals. It wasn't supposed to happen. After Scotland's first two games, the loss to Peru and the draw with Iran, the team had misfired, and it was all building up to this climatic thirty seconds of action and hope, when what we really needed was hope to be spread over all three games. Scotland was a very fashionable nation back then, the period just after the Bay City Rollers. I moved to London at that time, during the punk years, and there were lots of English people who supported Scotland. They just didn't like England at all. And people overseas liked Scotland, the tartan, the fashion, and the passion of it all. There was great pride in the national team but it all came to an end in the eighties in large part due to the sectarianism of Celtic and Rangers in Glasgow—Celtic's increasing identification with Ireland and Rangers with England.

In the last thirty years, Scotland has gone from the stature of being up there with Holland, to being down there with Northern Ireland. It's been an incredible, unremitting fucking downward slope since 1978, an all-encompassing secular decline; a lack of self-confidence. If Scotland were an independent country, the football would improve for a variety of reasons. Firstly, confidence would return, as Scotland would now be a nation, instead of a statelet. A Scottish government would probably invest a lot more in football. At the very least they would have an inquiry: how can we be so obsessed with something, and be so fucking bad at it? It defies all logic.

The first time I saw a football match on a big screen was during the 1982 World Cup in Spain. I was at Jimmy O'Rourke's place in Edinburgh. He had a three-light projector, one of those early ones. It was actually quite a good picture. It was during the Russia v Scotland game and there was this old guy not holding back, cursing every move by Graem, making e Souness, the Scotland midfielder. "He's preened his way through this fucking game. He's fucking rubbish," he said. I remember saying to Jimmy O'Rourke, "This old boy has it in for Souness." "That's his dad," was the reply.

In France '98, I was over there in Paris, and I watched the Scotland v Brazil opening game on one of the big screens set up outdoors. Here were two great football philosophies coming together. A pal of mine who worked in the music industry was planning a party with Kate Moss and all these other models later that night in the city. He gave me a call with the plans to meet up. I was on my way there, but I ran into these guys from Leith. I said to them, "I'm just on my way to meet Kate Moss and all these beautiful Parisian models," but they said, "Fuck them—you're having a drink wi' us." About five missed calls later, I was staggering around Paris singing "Flower of Scotland" with them.

Irvine Welsh All-Time World Cup XI

Dino Zoff

Carlos Alberto

Franz Beckenbauer

Fabio Cannavaro

John Blackley

Pat Stanton

Günter Netzer

Johan Cruyff

Diego Maradona

Pelé

Schillaci

Player Profile:
Tim Howard

illustration by Liu Yuhua

Birth Date:
June 3, 1979

Birth Place:
North
Brunswick,
USA

Height: 6'3"

Weight:
210 lbs.

Position:
Goalkeeper

DOG: Clayton

TATTOOS:
Superman's logo, mother's name, dragons, a cross, Chinese characters representing God, family, faith, health, and happiness

PERSONAL SONG CHANTED BY FANS:
(drunkenly sung to the tune of "Chim Chim Cheree," from the musical *Mary Poppins*)
Tim-Timmony Tim-Timmony Tim Tim Terroo...

QUOTE:
"I am who I am, and for me I'm quite happy with it."

NICKNAME: T-Ho

New Jersey's own T-Ho rocketed onto the world stage when he became the first American to win the English FA Cup with Manchester United. Going from being a teenager with the New York Metro Stars to making the English PFA's Team of the Year in 2004 is kind of like going from acting in Oklahoma at the Hohokus Repertory Theatre to winning an Oscar in a Martin Scorsese movie with George Clooney, Brad Pitt, Tom Cruise, Will Smith, Catherine Zeta-Jones and Angelina Jolie.

Now imagine doing all this with Tourette syndrome, a disorder that causes involuntary tics, and sometimes profane vocalizations. While playing for a notoriously Scottish manager who tolerates mistakes like Tony Soprano forgives those who trespass against you. While toiling in a media toilet with the British press like a pack of rabid jackals ripping your throat out.

T-Ho first donned the red, white, and blue in 2002, with a spark-ling debut shutout against Ecuador. And he had a crackerjack of a game against Mexico on the road to World Cup 2010, despite being savagely assaulted in the sanctuary of his goal box. He would love nothing more than to duplicate those heroics in 2010 in South Africa.

RIVALRY &
GRUDGE CO.
PURVEYORS OF
THE FINEST MATCHES
AND DIE-HARD
ANTAGONISM

¡A GANARLE A LOS GRINGOS!

USA VS.
LATIN AMERICA
EDITION

The rivalry between Mexico and the United States is one of the fiercest on the planet. When these two meet, it's the big enchilada, and the fouling is *más picante*. Just ask the American forward Cobi Jones. At the 2002 World Cup Finals, Mexico's Rafael Marquez, head-butted the American ace into next week. Every American player has felt Mexican cleats on their ass, legs, and bollocks. But the Yanks have learned to give it out, and not just on the field. US ace Landon Donovan allegedly said, "They are jealous of us, the Mexican players, because we've got a life and they have nothing. Because of that, they despise us." Ouch.

26

Things can get superstitious. Before a 2010 World Cup qualifier, a Mexican newspaper handed out voodoo dolls of Uncle Sam to any lapsed Catholic with a pin. During the game, the USA team dugout was pelted with trash. Urine bombs were also popular.

Besides Mexico, Spanish-speaking countries to the south regularly join in the fun. When the Yanks played El Salvador in 2009, they suffered a bad night's sleep at their hotel, thanks to loud music being blasted at 3 a.m. Rumors of phone calls to the US players' rooms at 4:30 a.m. added to the grumpiness. During the game, the stadium PA blasted air-raid-style sirens whenever El Salvador went on the attack. The Americans must have imagined themselves to be in a war.

THE UNITED STATES OF AMERICA

VS.

LATIN AMERICA

From the Alamo to today

When other attacks against the U.S. fell short, Mexico resorted to utilizing the Uncle Sam voodoo doll method.

UNDERDOGS: USA

The Game of Their Lives
Brazil '50

It's a funny old game. When the cousins met in the 1950 Finals in Brazil, the older boys were supposed to spank the younger ones, and teach them a lesson in the art of soccer. After all, America was the land of baseball, and host to a football game without the feet. England was the King of Soccer, the nation that forged the game. But in the heat of that historic Brazilian day in June, the aristocracy was in for a nasty jolt. The American rebels supplied the shock.

Joe Gaetjens scored the winner in the first half but the real hero of the game was US goalie Frank Borghi. Time and again he popped up like a jumping jack to deny the England attack. The English loss was a real smack in the face, and was warmly applauded by every country. English arrogance had ignored the first three World Cups, most likely out of fear. With the sun setting on its Empire, England was forced to face the facts. They were not the best anymore. Britannia didn't rule after all.

Sadly, the American heroes of 1950 were largely forgotten. There was no call from the President, no invite to the White House, no tickertape parade. The US media ignored soccer. It was foreign. It would be forty years until the Americans qualified for the Finals again.

AMERICAN SOCCER:

★ A Coming-of-Age Story ★

Over the years, many have tried to import soccer to America, as they have imported champagne, luxury automobiles, and designer cocaine. But as each wave of soccer has broken on the American shore, there has been an avalanche of vitriolic, barbaric knee jerking from the old guard of the US press. From the arrival of soccer gods Pelé and Beckenbauer in the seventies, to the invasion of marketing master and excellent bender of balls David Beckham, American sportswriters have mostly ground their axes on soccer. They say soccer is boring because people aren't constantly scoring touchdowns, runs, or baskets; that soccer players are effete pansy flowers who fall down in fake agony like they've been crippled when struck by a stiff wind; that they kiss when they celebrate and therefore almost certainly fellate each other.

It seems only appropriate that it's been the fairer sex that has embraced the beautiful game. In the words of the late, great soccer fanatic Jim Morrison, the men don't know but the little girls understand. It helps, of course, that the United States women delivered a World Cup championship, while their male counterparts haven't even sniffed one. Didn't hurt that in her moment of triumph, Lady Brandi whipped her top off and flashed her sports bra (along with some truly spectacular abs) at the world. A gener-

29

ation of girls were instantly converted, and filled the fields of America with soccer, dreaming of becoming the next Mia Hamm.

At this point a generation of American kids have grown up playing soccer. They don't see it as a foreign game owned by a bunch of greasy, unwashed, fornication-crazed immigrants. So more and more American athletes are kicking balls instead of throwing or hitting them. But until American men win a World Cup, soccer will never compete with baseball, basketball, or "football." Barring a miracle along the lines of the United States hockey team kicking Russia's ass, Jesus turning wine into a goal, or Allah slotting a corner kick through the eye of a needle, America will not win the World Cup in South Africa in 2010.

But picture, if you will, Team USA with linebacker Ray Lewis and a juiced-up Alex Rodriguez doling out punishment as center backs; Tom Brady and Derek Jeter running the midfield engine; and Kobe Bryant and Lebron James as twin center forwards penetrating even the most savvy and nasty defenses the world has to offer. Close your eyes and imagine those Americans hoisting the World Cup trophy aloft in victory and setting off a worldwide frenzy. Not so terribly far-fetched, is it?

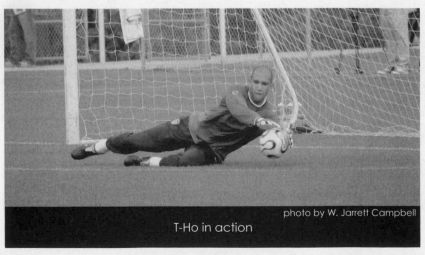

photo by W. Jarrett Campbell

T-Ho in action

When the white man first came to what is now the United States of America, he found a land teeming with tribes full of natives who lived in harmony with the land. The locals were master hunters and gatherers, and fierce, devout and highly skilled soccer players. The Cherokee, Cheyenne, Blackfoot and many others had excellent soccer squads. They called the game *pasuckuakohowog*, which means "beautiful game played with feet of the horse, wings of the eagle, heart of the mountain lion, and blood of the beaver, where the losers have their hearts cut out, and the winners eat them, covered in glory." That is a rough translation. In fact, at Plymouth Rock, when the Native Americans first encountered the Pilgrims, they introduced them to corn, pumpkin, and overlapping outside fullbacks. The very first recorded soccer match was held on what is now called Thanksgiving, because everyone was giving thanks that they were playing.

The United States was the first nation outside the UK to establish national rules and an organization to govern their fanatical soccer devotees. In 1862 the Oneida Football Club was born in Boston, and became the first American soccer superpower. The first official white man's soccer game was played on November 6, 1869, between Rutgers and Princeton. In 1873, a group of closeted, dandified aristobrats who called themselves the Eton Players came to New Haven to play Yale, in the first Anglo-American international soccer match. Many accounts

It's our favorite concept—you'll never play cricket again.

31

of the event suggest it was a continuation of the Boston Tea Party. Apparently the Yanks spanked the Etonians on their effete bums, and the Brits liked it.

Gradually, the American upper classes turned their backs on soccer, and immigrants from all over the world stepped in to fill the breach. In 1884, the American Football Association was created by a bunch of British ex-pats in Newark, New Jersey, now known for its industrial waste and urban decay. In 1885, the national soccer team played its very first game. And thus began a long tradition of losing games they should've won, when they were stomped by Canada, 1-0.

Coach Bob Bradley (*left*)

photo by David Sterry

Sam's Army

S am's Army was born on June 11, 1995, in Foxboro, Mass-achusetts. Many who were there swear on the lives of their loved ones that the face-painted, Cat in the Hat headgear-wearing, costume-festooned fanatics were singularly responsible for the thrilling historic 3-2 subjugation of fierce Nigeria.

If you haven't done so yet, do yourself a favor and go early to the next US national soccer team game in your area. Then follow your nose. You may smell a roasting pig or grilling beef, maybe the pungent sweetness of burning herb. You will probably hear music and perhaps chants as you get closer to the origin of the alluring aromas. You will almost certainly hear the sounds of passion and happiness, and feel the vibe of ridiculous optimism. When you arrive you will find yourself observing the ancient tribal art of tailgating, Sammer-style. There's a very good chance you will be invited to join the festivities. And you may well be offered an alcoholic beverage.

Many times when the US national team plays in its own mother country, it can seem like an away game. Mainly because so many fans in the stadium are rooting for the opposing team. That's why it's up to all of us to follow the example of Sam's Army, and show up in droves with our drums, our whistles, and our full-throated voices. Whether at home, or in South Africa, America absolutely needs a twelfth man.

Uruguay 1930

Although hardly anyone knows this, USA stood the world on its ear in the very first World Cup. Granted, the United States team fielded zero US-born players. But they opened several cans of whupass on Belgium and Paraguay, winning their group with a 6-0 aggregate. In the semifinals a cold Argentine slap of reality brought the US plummeting back to Earth. First the gauchos broke American center half Raphael Tracey's leg in the tenth minute. Then they just kept pouring salt in the wound, and when the dust settled, it was 6-1.

Italy 1934

In the 1934 World Cup, Team USA traveled to the boot of Europe and got a severe kicking. The haughty Italians lopped off their manhood so viciously, USA soccer went into hiding for thirteen years. The tournament started well enough with a solid qualifying win over Mexico, strongman Aldo "Buff" Donelli bagging four goals. But in the first round tie against Italy at Mussolini's Fascist Party stadium in Rome, the Italians savaged the Americans 7-1, sending them away.

Brazil 1950

Finally, the USA poked its head out from underneath the blanket, and made its way to the Finals in the Southern hemisphere. And the English were waiting for them. No one gave the States any hope. Only one US journalist was on hand to presumably cover the loss. His editor back home believed he had misreported the score, assuming England had won by a single goal—a huge shock in itself, as England had been pegged to put at least ten goals past US goalie Frank Borghi. But the famous victory over the colonial granddad (see page 28) was not enough to see the USA progress. Losses to

Spain and Chile booked the early berth home, back to hiding under the blanket, this time for forty years.

Italy 1990

In that forty-year hiatus, soccer rolled through the seventies craziness of the North American Soccer League (NASL) with its wacky uniforms and fading stars. The game became a novelty toy and was finally smashed to pieces in 1984 when the NASL folded. A Renaissance was due. Rumor has it that FIFA was desperate to have the United States host the World Cup in 1994. But everyone knew, for that to happen, they had to at least compete in Italy in World Cup 1990. There followed some dark chicanery that intensified the bitter hatred of the United States by Mexico, one of America's chief rivals for a spot in the Finals. Suddenly, our neighbor to the south was given a mysterious red card, disqualified from World Cup 1990 for using overage players at the 1989 World Youth Cup. Foul was cried, in Spanish, from Guadalajara to Tijuana. Conspiracy freaks screamed Mexico was reamed but as usual FIFA left no trace of its burglary.

Even with a stacked deck, Team USA had a miserable 1989, as they tried desperately to qualify for Italy '90. They were unorganized, sluglike and in general completely useless. When they were playing Costa Rica in St. Louis, a soccer hotbed, the announcer begged the fans to cheer. They steadfastly refused. It all came down to a final game against Trinidad and Tobago. With their backs to the wall, in a nail-biter of the highest order, Paul Caligiuri scored a spectacular goal that won the game for the USA, 1-0. It was massive. Team USA was back on the world soccer stage.

Their first game in World Cup 1990 was against an excellent Czechoslovakia squad. Team USA got their asses handed to them, 5-1. The team was "humiliated to the point of embarrassment" according to the *New York Times*. The television coverage was rubbish, the commentators explaining the rules through a basketball prism, and cutting away to a live interview with US goalie Tony Meola's mom, in the stands during the match. In the final two games, the team weren't horrible against host Italy, or against Austria, but that didn't change the fact that they were three and done. Back home, few seemed to care.

USA 1994

FIFA got its way. The United States was selected to host the 1994 World Cup, and the beautiful game came to the USA, whether she wanted it or not. The powers that be were hungry for the Yankee dollar, even though a survey taken before the tournament indicated that almost 75 percent of Americans did not even know what the World Cup was, and of those that did, 94 percent didn't give a flying f***. While the whole thing did make money, there were many complaints about $500 press passes, and outrageous fees for everything. And the opening ceremony was a joke. Sadly, America was the butt. Oprah Winfrey's was at the bottom of it, acting as emcee. Adding injury to insult, another soccer icon, Diana Ross, made an appearance. She attempted to kick the ball, and made a complete mockery of herself, and her country. But on the field, Team USA mercifully acquitted itself quite well, tying Switzerland 1-1, and putting a tremendous scare into eventual champions Brazil. But it is their second game that will always be remembered. They beat Colombia but at a terrible price. The winning score was an own goal by Colombian defender Andrés Escobar, who was tragically murdered as a result. (See page 52.)

Even though the US didn't advance, and despite the fact that most Americans seemed to vacillate between shrugging their shoulders with indifference, and lashing out in anger at the beautiful game, the seeds for development were sewn, and Major League Soccer was born.

France 1998

The United States finished last, including a loss to Iran. 'Nuff said.

Korea/Japan 2002

During the bleak 1998 campaign, one tiny light flickered. His name was Brian McBride. By Korea/Japan '02, he was part of a bright constellation of stars, including Reyna, Donovan and Friedel. Using thrusting wing play, the USA shot down Portugal, and then bombed Mexico out of the tournament, to reach the last eight. Germany committed the robbery in the quarterfinal, aided by a blind referee who missed a blatant penalty, a German handball on the goal line. Home again early but this time America had made its mark, and countries everywhere knew that the USA were a team to be reckoned with.

Germany 2006

After the success of 2002, there were huge expectations in the States for a repeat performance, but anticlimax is the curse of soccer and Team USA flapped around like a wet squib on a cold barbecue. The game's popularity in the US was exploding, and millions tuned in to be disappointed. The Czechs booked their way to an easy win over the US, and Ghana added another scar. Consolation came in a tie with eventual winners Italy. In some ways, the humdrum exit was progress as it stopped the swing from the highs to the extreme lows of previous tournaments. Balance had set on American expectations. And this has helped the team settle and mature through a solid performance in the Confederations Cup in 2009.

photo by W. Jarrett Campbell

39

LANDON DONOVAN

Landon Donovan has become the face of American soccer. An ace striker with an uncanny knack of being in the right place at the right time. A patriot's player, he'll fight to the end for the red, white and blue. And he's not shy about his opinions. Last year, he called out David Beckham publicly, accusing the man who married Posh Spice of being a whining, malignant ingrate. Many agreed and admired him for his honesty.

Donovan, all laid-back with the Jamaican team.

photo by Michael Kane

JOZY ALTIDORE

Josmer Volmy Altidore to be exact. Could he be the real deal? Many have been called, but few have been chosen, in America's relentless search for an international world-class goal scorer. On

April Fools' Day, 2009, the Jersey-born striker became the youngest American to score an international hat trick, when he got all jiggy against Trinidad and Tobago. His magnificent combination of brute strength and artiste touch carries him over defenders. A major threat to foreign defenses in South Africa 2010.

CLINT DEMPSEY

photo by Michael Kane

From a Texas trailer park to the dizzying heights of world soccer, Clint Dempsey has earned a reputation as one cool customer. After being named MLS Rookie of the Year, he flirted with Dutch giants Feyenoord, before signing with English squad Fulham, for the biggest transfer fee any American had ever procured. He has not disappointed, becoming a local hero at the West London club. In addition to scoring the quickest goal in US national team history, when he netted against Barbados fifty-three seconds into a game, he ran riot in the Confederations Cup, first scoring the historic goal that sent Team USA into its first-ever FIFA final, then shocking mighty mighty Brazil with a spectacular opening goal. He was awarded the Bronze Ball. An inspirational player. Top drawer.

NATIONAL TEAM COACH: BOB BRADLEY

Yet another product of the soccer machine that is New Jersey, he began his coaching career as a wunderkind, taking over Ohio University at the ripe old age of twenty-two. From there, he was snapped up by the University of Virginia by a man who would become instrumental in his rise to the top of American soccer: Bruce Arena.

After a brief stint at his alma mater, Princeton, Bruce came calling again, and Bob joined him at DC United. After World Cup 2006, Bruce Arena handed over the reins of the national team to his protégé. Leading the USA to the Final of the Confederations Cup in 2009, proved his leadership mettle. His son Michael is a regular on the US national team, and paid tribute to Dad by scoring a goal on Father's Day during the tournament.

OGUCHALU CHIJIOKE ONYEWU

Nigerian parents, citizen of both Belgium and the United States, and the tallest outfield player in the history of

photo by Michael Kane

Gooch (number 5) using his head

Team USA, Gooch, as he is known, has become the rock in America's defense. He stepped into the large redheaded shoes of US soccer legend Alexi Lalas, when he became the second American to play in Italy's prestigious Serie A, signing with AC Milan. Solid in the tackle, and brilliant in the air, expect Gooch to provide the backbone for success in South Africa.

CARLOS BOCANEGRA

After being named MLS Rookie of the Year, and two-time Defender of the Year, Bocanegra bolted to that sanctuary for Yankees in the English Premier League, Fulham, where Brian McBride made his bones. This led to a transfer to Rennes, where he played with style and panache, scoring a classic UEFA Cup goal while he was at it. He has become a mainstay for Team USA, and even served as captain during the historic ass kicking America gave to European champions Spain in South Africa in 2009.

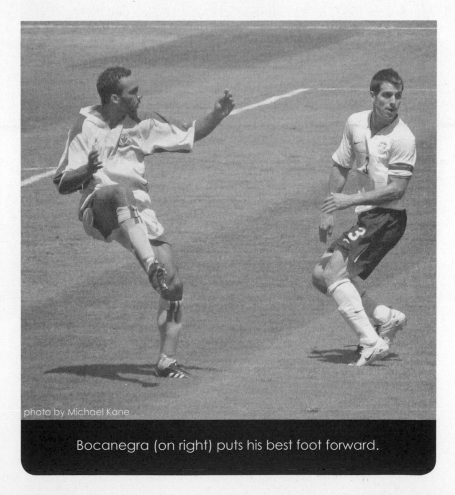

photo by Michael Kane

Bocanegra (on right) puts his best foot forward.

COBI JONES

Mr. Jones is still the most-capped soccer player in the history of the country. His speed, industry, charisma and fearlessness, along with his crazy dreadlocked head, earned him a well-deserved reputation as one of the best and most popular soccer players America has produced. He is the only American who has played in both the English Premier League and the Brazilian First Division. After Copa America in 1995, he earned the nickname El Escobillón.

ERIC WYNALDA

For many years Eric was both the top-scoring player in US history, and the first US player to be red carded from a World Cup match. A scrappy fighter with a nose for goal, he was never one to hold his tongue. Although he served Team USA proudly and well for many seasons, in recent years he gained massive notoriety when he viciously attacked fellow ESPN commentator Jim Rome, a known idiot and constant disparager of soccer, saying publicly that Mr. Rome could, "suck my d*ck." Right on, Eric!

ALEXI LALAS

Panayotis Alexander Lalas was once described in the *New York Times* as "a heavy-metal Ronald McDonald." His head-banging, guitar-playing, wild-style hair and crazy red goatee earned him a rabid cult following. At the height of his popularity, droves of fanatics sported red fright wigs and fake facial hair in tribute to their guitar hero. Although some dismissed him as a one-man traveling circus, he was actually a brutal and useful defender, a terrific header of a ball, and still the only player in the history of the United States national soccer team to have opened for Hootie & the Blowfish.

BRIAN MCBRIDE

Another product of the American soccer factory at St. Louis University, the only thing Brian McBride ever did, everywhere he went, was score goals. He became such a popular player at his club Fulham, a bar inside the stadium was renamed "McBride's" in his honor. He is also central to one of the most enduring images of American courage, when he played in a blood-soaked bandage, after being savagely attacked by cowardly Italian Daniele de Rossi in World Cup 2006. De Rossi was banned and fined. Brian McBride, on the other hand, was bloodied but unbowed. A true American soccer hero.

Brian McBride — a great American footballer

photo by Michael Kane

The Road to the World Cup 2010: America Doesn't Suck After All
by David Sterry

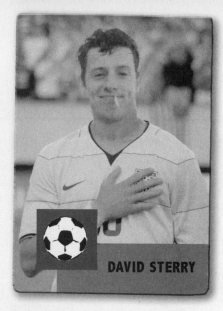

DAVID STERRY

ings of thievery, abductions, and murder, claiming there was was no way South Africa could put on a world-class event. While South Africa herself was promising to put on a jungle drum-fueled, vuvuzela-blowing, Euro-samba, Anglo-Asian blowout of global proportion.

This was the atmosphere when a poor, pitiful, rag-tag Team USA showed up to throw down against a galaxy of Goliaths: 2006 champions Italy; world numero uno Spain; and mighty Brazil. Armed without even a slingshot, based on a recent mauling at the hands of Costa Rica, where they played like a bunch of soccer moms.

One year exactly from when the world was set to invade South Africa, the Confederations Cup was an intensely scrutinized dress rehearsal. It would be the last big international tournament before the mother of them all, the World Cup, crash-landed in the mother of all continents, Africa, for the first time in history. Cynics and skeptics all over the planet were sharpening their blades, with warn-

It's been hard to be American for quite some time. When you go into a bar anywhere in the world and say you're American, people often look at you like you just tried to kill their dog. But if you are a member of the American national soccer team, you have felt hated for decades. Foreign fans throw coins, batteries, even baggies full of warm piss at you. Worse, you've been the object of pity, the butt of jokes. So often you have just plain sucked. Sure, every once in a while Team America would make a little splash. And we have come to dominate what is a weak sister region of the soccer world. But time and time again, when we come up against the big boys, we have turned from men into mice.

So, as America opened up against Italy, they seemed nervous, shaky, and insecure; like a homeowner six months behind on the mortgage. For one brief shining moment there was a ray of hope, as the penalty machine himself, golden boy Landon Donovan, slotted home a penalty kick. Shockingly, America had a lead. Before you could say badda bing badda boom, they were drowning in wave after wave of pressure from men with vowels at the ends of their names. Suddenly Italy was up 3-1. But it wasn't just the

fact that Team America was was slapped so badly. It was the fact that they looked like a mediocre college team trying to play against the Yankees. The salt in the wound came courtesy of two brilliantly taken goals scored by a guy from New Jersey. Because his parents happen to be Italian, he got to choose which country to play for. He chose Italy over us. Bastard.

That's when the nightmare really began. Because next up were the kings of soccer, the team that puts the beautiful in the beautiful game, Brazil. Sure enough, the samba masters toyed with the red, white and blue like an alpha cat with three blind mice. The low point was when Brazil scored on an American corner kick. The final score was 3-0. If not for T-Ho, the indomitable goalkeeper Tim Howard, the score could have been 10-0.

A great cry was heard on the World Wide Web: Fire Coach Bradley! He is homegrown, not a fancy foreign import, like Chevy versus Mercedes-

Benz. And, he is untested on the world stage. Plus, his son plays almost every minute of every game. And recently his son had been skinned, turned inside out by an attacker, made to look like a rank pantywaisted amateur. The heat was on. America had one game left, against Egypt. There was a tiny, slim, infinitesimal chance that Team USA could still qualify for the next round. But judging by how badly they had blown, the fat lady was warming up to sing.

Then something strange happened. America started being...well...America. The boys worked harder, ran more, and threw their bodies around with reckless abandon. They left their hearts, guts, and nuts out on the field. You bust your ass, you play with mad passion, and all of a sudden you get a lucky break. Funny how that happens in life, eh? How lucky? News came. Brazil was running roughshod over the suddenly hapless Italians. If Brazil could finish three goals ahead, and America could do the same, the miracle would be manifest, and the USA would be through to the next round. Nose to grindstone, pedal to metal, fingers to bone, America scrapped and clawed. And suddenly there was Micheal Bradley, son of the coach, stroking the ball home like an old pro. Scoring a goal for his old man on Father's Day. Word came in that Brazil had spanked the haughty Italians sufficiently. America needed one more goal. They needed a hero. That was when Clint "Eastwood" Dempsey made America's day, streaking into the goalmouth, muscling a header past the traumatized Egyptian goalkeeper.

The Spanish and their soccer Armada were now on the horizon, the number one soccer team in the world. A bunch of pretty, pampered, delicate genius multimillionaires who recently won the European Championship. But the USA came out guns blazing, Devil may care glint in the eye, a jaunty Stars & Stripes spring in the step. The Spaniards sincerely believed all they had to do was throw their sweetly scented jockstraps out onto the field, and the uncultured, uncouth, uncool Americans would bow down before them. But the Americans, breathing fire from their belly, chased and harried like hungry pack animals looking to feed. Their naked aggression seemed to offend the sweet geniuses of Spain. Time and again, when they were tackled and stripped nude of the ball, they stood and pouted like sulking children.

And then there was Jozy "the Pussycat" Altidore being fed the ball at the top of the penalty box. In every contact sport there is that mano a mano moment where it becomes one man's strength against another's. It's caveman primal. Can I beat you down? Or will you beat me down? The Pussycat proved to be the better man, kicking sand in the face of the feeble Spaniard, like he was a 98-pound weakling. Having bested his foe, the Pussycat took his sweet time, set his sights, locked and loaded, and pulled the trigger. 1-0. The world bugged its eyes, palms outstretched as if to say, "OH MY GOD!"

Wave after wave of the Spanish Armada tried to land on American shores. But each time, led by Gooch Onyewu, the attacks were thwarted. Once again, T-Ho was a God, repelling attacks with a fierce animal agility.

There's an old rule of love and war. When you attack from the front, you leave your back door open. And the increasingly frantic Spaniards did just that, committing forces willy-nilly up front, while their unprotected ass was sticking right up in the air. And there was Landon Donovan, with the golden boy luster, driving with the ball at his feet, making things happen, putting in nasty little crosses. Still, the Spaniards had the situation well in hand. Except for two things—their arrogance, and good old American never-say-quit. Clint "Eastwood" Dempsey, this time like a sneak thief in the night, nipped in from behind a gilded Spanish defender, who, thinking he had all the time in the world because he was so rich, talented, and dashingly handsome, had casually trapped the ball right in front of his own goal. With some serious foot-is-quicker-than-the-eye action, Clint had the ball in the Spanish net before the Spaniards could say ay caramba! Team America had made it to the final of the Confederations Cup. Now all they had to do was put away mighty Brazil.

The Americans were cocky as a horned-up college student on a date that he knows is going to end up with him getting lucky. Boldly knocking the ball around, defending with calm assurance, attacking intelligently and economically. America was playing like…well…Brazil. Even more shockingly, Brazil was playing like America at her worst. Giving the ball away sloppy, passing the ball to no one in particular. Then in the blink of an eye, there he was again, Dempsey. With a silky, delicate, world-class touch, he massaged the ball into the Brazilian net like a tantric master. USA 1. Brazil 0. And they deserved it.

Naturally Brazil brought it hard and heavy. But the USA stood strong. And once again, when you attack from the front, you leave the back door open. It was Donovan Time. He made a monkey out of the Brazilian defense, and like a lion ripping the jugular of an antelope, he slammed the ball home, triggering a wild red, white and blue celebration.

But as soon as the second half started, Brazil demonstrated why they're Brazil. Out of nowhere, out of nothing, a quick Brazilian pirouette followed by a slashing shot from Fabiano, and America was digging the ball out of their net.

This is where USA teams of yore would have folded like a house of crooked cards, but not this team. They didn't panic. They didn't freak out. They kept defending. They kept attacking. And all the while, T-Ho the Magnificent was a true tower of power, near post, far post, and everywhere in between. He even showed some excellent acting skills, convincing everyone he had saved a Brazilian header, which clearly crossed the goal line.

Although he was robbed of an Oscar, he was named Goalkeeper of the Tournament.

But Brazil is, after all, Brazil. They find a way. Brazil 3. USA 2. The final whistle blew. But Team USA showed that we could play with the big boys. We turned from mice into men right before the world's eyes. At World Cup 2010, we're going to bring everything we've got. And in our hearts, we know that with a little luck, we can be the Cinderella, who ends up with the glass slipper in South Africa.

David Sterry All-Time World Cup XI

Dino Zoff

Bobby Moore

Franz Beckenbauer

Roberto Carlos

Johan Cruyff

Zinedine Zidane

Dunga

Diego Maradona

Eusébio

Gerd Müller

Pelé

VILLAINS

MADNESS

VIOLENCE   DEATH

HUMBERTO MUÑOZ CASTRO

Señor Castro was sentenced to forty-three years in prison for murdering Colombian defender Andrés Escobar, the hapless defender who scored an own goal during the 1994 Finals. Escobar may have been spared the bullet if his own goal had been for any other country but the United States.

He was gunned down leaving a restaurant with his girlfriend. The twelve shots on target were accompanied by a dozen yells of "Goal." Rumor suggested the assassin's bosses had lost a large chunk of change because of Escobar's blunder.

Castro was sentenced to forty-three years for the murder but was released early for good behavior. Some in Colombia reckoned eleven years was enough for killing a player who helped bundle his team out of the tournament. Colombian soccer never fully recovered. They faded from international acclaim. The coaches found it difficult to find confident central defenders ready to take over Escobar's position. The great fear of the own goal unhinged the security of the entire team, and the nation.

 DEATH   VIOLENCE   ALCOHOL   DRUGS   MADNESS   NUDITY   INSULT   TERRORISM

photo by Ryu Voelkel

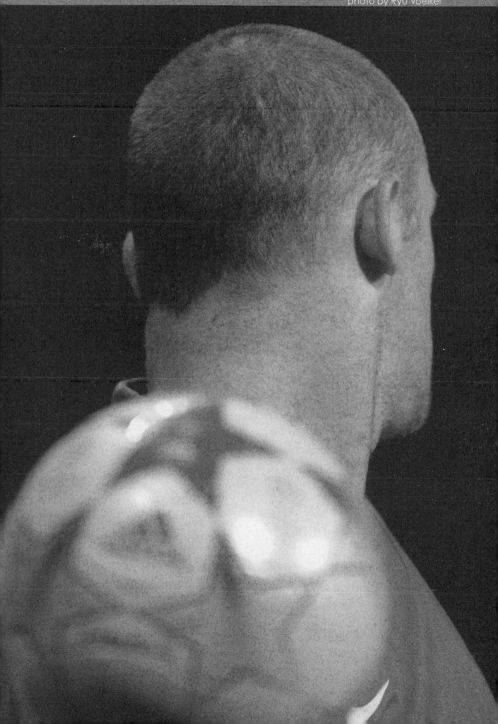

Wayne Rooney

illustration
by Liu Yuhua

BORN:
Oct. 24, 1985
Liverpool, England

HEIGHT: 5'10"

WEIGHT:
175 lbs.

POSITION: Striker

NICKNAME: Wazza

QUOTE:
"Sometimes you need to look inside yourself."

NEWSPAPERS ROONEY READS: None.

FAVORITE FILM: *Dumb and Dumber*

FAVORITE FOODS: corndogs, sausages, chips and
baked beans

TATTOOS:
Cross, Colleen, Just Enough Education To Perform

WORST MOMENT: Attempted castration of Portugal's Carvalho in World Cup 2006

PERSONAL SONG CHANTED BY FANS:
"He's fat, he's Scouse, he'll rob your f*cking house, It's Wayne Rooney, Wayne Rooney."

He was first spotted at the age of nine by a scout. Wayne Rooney shot like a cannonball into the firmament of English soccer when he became the youngest goal scorer in the Premiership with a mind-blowing, world-class wonder goal against Arsenal. He was sixteen at the time. Soon thereafter, his star shot across an even wider swath of the heavens when he became the youngest player ever to pull on the three Lions jersey, debuting for England 111 days after he turned seventeen. Naturally, this pugnacious prodigy became the youngest goal scorer in the history of England when he rudely violated the goal of Macedonia. Roo-mania then swept relentlessly through the UK.

Wayne possesses a rare combination of brute strength, bulldog tenacity, fearless and dominant ability, and magical skills. Rooney is also a world-class swearer, and during one tirade, it was unofficially estimated that he spouted twenty profanities at a referee in under a minute. He is married to his childhood sweetheart. Like him, love him, or loathe him, Wayne Rooney makes a habit of scoring large and spectacular goals when his team most needs them. And England will certainly need them in South Africa in 2010.

Country Profile:
England

That's who we are! And we're tired of waiting. We invented the queue in England—at the post office, waiting for surgery, signing on the dole. And now we're at the head of the line. So world, get behind us, where you belong; the Union Jacks will be putting their hands on that golden trophy soon enough.

You geezers keep saying the sun has set on the British Empire. And it might seem so considering we've won nothing for almost half a century. But history is long in Her Majesty's Realm and we can wait until we return to South Africa. And leading the charge will be our Wayne Rooney. Wazza's a pedigree chum of the highest bulldog order. And Rooney is going to go loony scoring goals in Africa.

Sure, the food is rank in England. So we've dumped the boiled beef and potatoes for a pukka plate of pasta. Fabio Capello is our Italian job, a manager who ranks up there with Sir Alf Ramsey, the leader of our glorious expedition in 1966. Signor Capello has the right ingredients to make South Africa into a Bolognese of English triumph. He has the look, the suits, and the spectacles.

We've got some of the hardest-looking footballers in decades. John Terry and Rio Ferdinand, guardians of the back door, they can bounce anyone out of the game. When they're not in the pub having ale, Frank Lampard and Stevie Gerrard are sweeping the midfield into top gear, and shifting it up front to the bulldog, and the likes of Theo Walcott. So be warned, enemies of Britannia. We will fight you on the beaches, and in the stands.

But topping it all are the profiles of our footballers' wives. They are the hottest and most beautiful WAGS, sunny side up. Shopping will be high on the agenda, and maybe a snap or two with Mrs. Beckham, if Fabio decides to take her old man along to make the tea. It's all biscuits, bangers, and breezy filler for us Brits. It keeps me wondering whom we'll beat in the Final.

ENGLAND FACTS

Founded: In the pub, 927 AD, just before last call
Population: 51 million and one Queen
Calling code: 44
Alcohol consumption: 51 million pints of beer a day
Emergency tel. #: 999
Language: English
Major cities: Newcastle, Birmingham, Leeds, Liverpool, Hull
Government: Constitutional Farce
World Heritage Site: Stonehenge-Neolithic beer kegs

RIVALRY &
GRUDGE CO.
PURVEYORS OF
THE FINEST MATCHES
AND DIE-HARD
ANTAGONISM

ARGENTINA VS.
ENGLAND
EDITION

It had been four years since Argentina and England had met on the battlefield. The two nations had warred over the tiny Falkland Islands in the South Atlantic. The islands' fields were saturated with Argentine and English blood. Argentina's dragon was slain by English mettle. But God had still to play his hand.

Match day was boiling hot. Revenge filled the Argentines. The English neck never looked juicier. Argentina's maestro, Diego Maradona, had sharpened his teeth and procured a manicure. The pale English players donned their armor, and cursed the Mexican sun god. The crowd was demented.

In the fifty-first minute, Maradona kicked Michelangelo off his stool, and painted his own Hand of God. He palmed the ball over England's goalie, into the net. The referee was struck blind. But Divine Intervention was captured for eternity on film. God had helped the cheat. And he was not finished with the English. Five minutes later, Maradona performed the miracle moves that became the Best Goal of the Twentieth Century. He slaughtered the English players in his journey towards the net. Rumor had it that the Pope crossed himself, on seeing the goal on television.

After the match, Maradona said, "Although we had said before the game that football had nothing to do with the Falklands war, we knew they had killed a lot of Argentine boys there, killed them like little birds. And this was revenge."

**ARGENTINA
vs.
ENGLAND**

Quarterfinal

June 22,
1986

Estadio
Azteca,
Mexico City

The fact that Maradona's hand knocked the ball into the goal went undetected by the referee.

photo by Ryu Voelkel

UNDERDOGS: NORTH KOREA

England '66

Not a lot of people know this. On the soccer field during England '66, North Korea invented the all-out attack. Their players blasted onto the world stage, erasing tournament favorites Italy, in their route to the quarterfinals. They remain a special charm in the underdog hall of fame.

The bus journey was long, from Pyongyang to Middlesborough in Northern England. There, the North Koreans set about showing the world that speed, fitness, and single-minded devotion to the cause paid off. Before giving them the bus fare, Kim Il-sung, the great leader of the nation, had this piece of sage Asian advice: "Win."

The people of Middlesborough, a forgotten English town, took the Reds to their hearts. The city's team played in the same colors, and the stadium was filled with locals in red scarves, the day the North Koreans bundled the heavily favored Italians out. With Italy reduced to ten men early on, the Koreans took full advantage. By halftime, they were leading by a single strike, a goal they would never surrender.

Their famous quarterfinal game against Portugal, which they lost 5-3, after leading 3-0, was played in "Beatlemania" Liverpool. Thousands of townsfolk from Middlesborough made the journey to support their new Korean friends. Britain and North Korea had no diplomatic relations. It was the Cold War. The Korean national anthem was banned from play before their games. But the burghers of Middlesborough would have gladly twinned with Pyongyang. North Korea in 1966 was one of the greatest giant killers of all-time.

North Korea

Fearless leader
Kim Jong-il
gearing up
for victory

NORTH KOREA FACTS

Capital: Pyongyang
Population: 22,666,000
Drive: On the right
Government: Stalinist-style cult
Currency: North Korea Won
Calling code: 850
Internet suffix: .kp
Armed Forces: 1.2 million uniforms
Nuclear Weapons: Yes, please.
National Pastime: Winning

A*n nyoung ha seh yo.* We heard that cult worship was popular with you weirdo Americans, but for us in North Korea, we do it better. The Big Daddy of our country is Kim Il-sung, founder of the nation, made President for Life, after he died. It matters not! His son, the Dear Small Fry, Kim Jong-il, has shown us how to make love to nuclear weapons, and expect nothing for breakfast, lunch and dinner. Some of us one day hope to own sunglasses like the Dear Leader. But the big news is not our empty plates, or our middle finger raised to the planet, but qualification for the World Cup in South Africa, after a forty-four-year hiatus.

The Chollima, the nickname of our national team, named after the winged horse, never stop running. Their gutsy gallop through the qualifiers proved that in the DPRK, we believe in endurance, courage, and disciplined haircuts. Built around our core defensive ideology, the spin-offs have produced amazing results. More solid than a brick outhouse, our centrifugal defense whips away threats. Our speedy attacks overwhelm opponents. Before you know it, we're in your penalty box, and the ball is flying at your goal like a missile on its way to Tokyo. It's all out with us, absolutely ruthless. And if you try and get in our way, we don't mind implementing the odd savage hack, or nuclear war.

In South Africa, North Korea is going to party like its 1966. We were the stuff of legend during the '66 Finals in England. Considered a joke, we soon wiped the smiles off the faces of the prima donna Italians, sending them home to Mama. Portugal suffered a heart attack in the quarterfinal. We were leading 3-0 at halftime only to lose 5-3 in the end. And how did we learn to shock? By inventing the all-out attack! Only our goalkeeper stayed in front of enemy lines, even at 3-0, the Chollima continued the full frontal flight at Portugal, refusing to defend. Our players returned to the homeland as national heroes. As a reward, they were given uniforms that were ironed, and forever revered as champions of the partisans, vanguards of the soccer revolution. The world got the message, and soon replaced their static soccer with our attacking frequencies. You can find the origins of Holland's 1970's Total Football style in North Korea '66. *Dedahnhee kamsahamnida.*

Your foreign bookmakers are showing the odds of North Korea taking the prize home to Pyongyang at 1000-1? Get ten of your bucks on it now. The Chollima are destined for glory. No barricade will get in our way. No line of foreign attack will breach our defense. And if we meet up with you pabo Americans, and beat you imperialists, the heavens will open and Big Daddy Kim Il-sung will swoop down on his winged horse, and take the players to the paradise of workers cooperatives, and factories in our Commie heaven.

Player Profile:
Park Ji-Sung

Liu Yuhua

BORN:
Feb. 25, 1981
Suwon,
Gyeonggi-do,
South Korea

HEIGHT: 5'9"

POSITION:
Midfielder

NICKNAME: Three-Lungs Park. New Engine

SONG: "Song for Park"

HOMETOWN TRIBUTE: A Street named after him:
Park Ji-Sung Road

QUOTE: "I may not be as handsome as David Beckham, but I hope, and believe, I can be just as good as he was."

HOBBY: Soccer video games.

BIGGEST ENEMY: Loneliness (being single and living 6,000 miles from home)

Park Ji-Sung is a classic case of David becoming Goliath. Born tiny, his father fed him exotic Asian delicacies such as boiled frog, hoping that his son would grow. Ji-Sung threw up, but he didn't grow much. After high school, he was told to piss off by many reputable professional sides, because he was too small. He finally latched onto a Division 2 team desperate enough to take a chance on this unknown undersized dynamo. He led them to a championship, which led to then South Korean national team coach Guus Hiddink making him an instrumental part of the World Cup 2002 squad. He scored the most monumental goal in the nation's soccer history, a crackerjack of a strike against Portugal, advancing South Korea historically into the semifinals. From there he was whisked to Holland, and from there to titan Manchester United, where he became the first Asian player to play in a European Cup final. At each step he was met with skepticism and mistrust. And in each case, he has won the hearts and minds of fans, critics and managers alike.

Park Ji-Sung is not the fastest. He's not the strongest. He's not the most skillful. And yet he has become one of the greatest soccer players in the history of Asia. How? By being the Energizer Bunny, running more, working harder, having more stamina, fitness, and endurance than anyone else on any pitch. That's how he got his nickname, Three-Lungs Park. He's the only player in history that legendary hardman manager Sir Alex Ferguson told, "Take out that battery! You're running far too much." There's no chance of not running enough when Park Ji-Sung leads South Korea into what what they hope will be a long stay in South Africa.

photo directly above by Stefan Meisel

The 2002 Finals in Korea and Japan

by Simon Kuper

(At the World Cup Finals, the <u>Financial Times</u> writer reflected on the exhaustion of covering the tournament.)

SIMON KUPER

It's Saturday so this may be Osaka, but I say that without conviction. Senegal-Turkey today will be my sixteenth game in twenty-one days and Lord knows how many cities.

We sometimes travel a distance comparable to London-Marseille to see a match, and then move on at six the next morning. Japan is a blur of rice fields and shopping malls seen through the windows of bullet trains. Annoyingly, when you try to while away the journey by checking e-mails from home, you find they say things such as: "I am soooooooooo jealous of you." Home is probably the best place to experience this hardest of World Cups. This is not just a journalist's whine: the competition is almost as tough on the players.

The theme tune of the 1990 World Cup was "Nessun Dorma." It is true that no one here sleeps much either. Four hours is normal but a more appropriate tune for this World Cup would be Paul Simon's "Homeward Bound."

It may have been in Sapporo that someone told me the story about the rock star on tour. Every day the rock star checked into a new hotel room, but after a while he began to suspect it was always the same room. He hit upon a rock-star-like solution: he broke the mirror in each of his rooms before leaving, so that when he arrived in the next one he would know he was somewhere new.

Unfortunately, another member of his band saw what he was doing. Arriving at the next hotel, this man hurried to his friend's room and smashed the mirror. When the rock star opened the door and saw the same broken mirror as the night before, he had a breakdown and had to go to hospital. The closest I have come to breakdown occurred in the Kakegawa Grand Hotel. I would like to explain where Kakegawa is, but I have no idea.

The best description of alienation I had ever heard until then came from a black American I met in a Prague bar soon after the fall of communism. This man had found himself teaching English somewhere in rural Slovakia where he

was not just the only black man within 100 miles, but also the only Westerner within 100 miles. He was all right for a while, he said, more or less coping, until he was attacked by a hedgehog and got on the first train to Prague. "I felt pretty alienated," he said.

So did I, alone in my ninth-floor room on four hours' sleep, in a place I could never find on a map, in a country where I cannot read a single symbol of its three alphabets. I wanted to go home, if only I could remember where that was.

But that was last week (I think). Since then I have had another night in the Kakegawa Grand — I could tell by the broken mirror and now it feels like home to me.

Like us, the players are not in Japan but in the World Cup. They live in sealed hotels where even the waiters have been brought from their own country. They get more sleep than us, but their bodies hurt more. They hardly ever get out, yet even they travel too much.

The night England beat Argentina in Sapporo, arguably the team's best result in twelve years, the English reserve defender Martin Keown was thinking of other things. "You've got to fly all over the place," he marveled. "You could be in England traveling to Spain for the time it's taken us to get down here." Keown meant "up here"—Sapporo is on an island north of Japan—but he is forgiven.

It is difficult for footballers to be sure they would rather be at the World Cup than home with their families. When a team wins a match, the nation back home might charge whooping on to the streets. But the players get on an aircraft, refuse a drink from a trolley, and check into their new hotel room at 4 a.m.

Footballers sometimes reveal years later that a World Cup was the unhappiest time of their lives. A training camp is rather like being in the army.

Colleagues can bully, and some worry about what their partners are getting up to at home.

Italy's Paolo Maldini missed his family so much he would watch them on a webcam. France's Zinedine Zidane flew to South Korea a couple of days after his wife gave birth. He cannot have been in the right mood for a World Cup.

I suspect alienation was one reason why Ireland's Roy Keane went home before the football began. On the night the Republic of Ireland qualified for the second round, earning themselves an aircraft journey from Japan to Korea, their winger Jason McAteer gave a bittersweet paean to his roommate Steve Staunton. "It's another week with Steve," McAteer laughed. "Half of me's hoping we'll get separate rooms in Seoul. No, he's great: another week listening to his conversations with his dad."

McAteer's teammate Steve Finnan admitted: "You're looking forward to going home. But obviously we

hope it will be after the final."
Yet I suspect that when Ireland
lost their second-round match
on penalties to Spain, some part
of every Irish player was thinking, "Hurrah, we're free!"

The French, Italians and
Argentines were too tired
for this World Cup. The winner
will be the last team left standing.

Simon Kuper All-Time World Cup XI

Ramón Quiroga

Phillip Cocu

Franco Baresi

Lilian Thuram

Benjamin Massing

Boudewijn Zenden

Falcão

Jan Ceulemans

Diego Maradona

Johnny Rep

Roger Milla

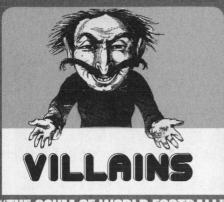

VILLAINS

INSULT VIOLENCE

"THE SCUM OF WORLD FOOTBALL"

Batista is a name associated with villainy in pre-Castro Cuba, and it is also the surname of a Uruguayan player who sits at the head table for World Cup criminals. Famously sent off after fifty-three seconds for committing grievous bodily harm against a Scottish opponent during a World Cup tie, José Batista earned his country the reputation of being "the scum of world football."

This ignoble attachment on an entire nation was uttered by the president of the Scottish Football Association after his country had been on the end of a Uruguayan beating. Their first round clash during Mexico '86 was a Darwinian example of brutality and machismo at its most devolved. Encouraged by Batista's example, scything Uruguayan tackles harvested the remaining Scotland players, and the match officials were threatened, cajoled, and in need of new underwear by the end of this frightful exhibition.

The Scottish vowed never to play Uruguay again, if they could help it. The tartan media suggested any Uruguayan living in Scotland should leave the country immediately. Fortunately, no Uruguayans had been stupid enough to move there in the first place. Luckily, the countries were at opposite ends of the planet, and the chance of war breaking out was limited to the soccer field. The memory of Batista's villainy has not faded. His hateful hack is a candidate for the most violent play in World Cup history.

DEATH VIOLENCE ALCOHOL DRUGS MADNESS NUDITY INSULT TERRORISM

THE HARDMEN

A LAMENT FOR THE BEAUTIFUL BRUTES

Blame the first ape man. Booting another monkey's testicles to steal his coconut devolved into robbing a team of its star player by neutering him with a savage hack. That was soccer. And there were key players executing this Darwinian selection, the survival of the fittest. Their reputations threw splatters on the canvas of the Beautiful Game. And we loved them for it.

Leonel Sánchez was Chile's answer to Genghis Khan. The son of a boxer, he broke the nose of an Italian in the filthiest World Cup game ever played, the infamous Battle of Santiago (see page 84). Decades later came Andoni Goikoetxea known as the "Butcher of Bilbao." In the eighties, the Spaniard's play littered the field with shattered shins, crumpled craniums, and axed ankles, but he always got the ball, except once. His brutal chop on Diego Maradona left the Argentine out of the game for months. Players trembled when their backs were to the goal, knowing that the Butcher was around with his knifing legs.

Meanwhile, across the Mediterranean playing in the boot of Italy, the incongruously named Claudio Gentile was nothing of the sort. His marking on opponents was as indelible as a permanent Sharpie. His dark shadow cast fear over his enemies; he tackled like an armored tank ramming a roadblock. Referees cowered before him.

72

He was never sent off. He is credited with securing Italy's passage to the World Cup Final in 1990, snuffing out the luckless Maradona. Undoubtedly, he was one of the greatest defenders of all time.

The Brits have a galaxy of choppers: from Nobby Stiles to Norman "Bite Yer Legs" Hunter to Stuart "Psycho" Pearce to Scotland hard man Graeme Souness. Pearce attacked players like Sid Vicious attacked fans with his bass guitar. He was the punk menace of English soccer for years, a brilliant defender with a rocket launcher for a left foot. Souness was a terrific midfielder, world class, and he hated losing, or drawing. He was willing to do anything to secure victory. His bullying style, broken nose, and macho mustache terrified grown men. He was the kind of guy that you feared bumping into in a bar's restroom. Even as a manager, he inflicted aggro on his enemies, famously planting his team's flag in the center circle of an opponent's stadium after a victory. Rioting ensued and ambulances were soon flying to the hospitals.

Sadly, today's game has become a regimen of correctness, with referees handing out cautions like candy. Hefty fines and bans for robust play have kept the hard man in the closet. Diving, faking injury, and crying wolf have undermined the hard tackle. The old phrase, "he marked him out of the match" is long gone. The-man-on man battle is fading away, while the new evangelism of prettiness has robbed the game of its beautiful brutes.

Carlos Tévez, Argentina

photo by Ryu Voelkel

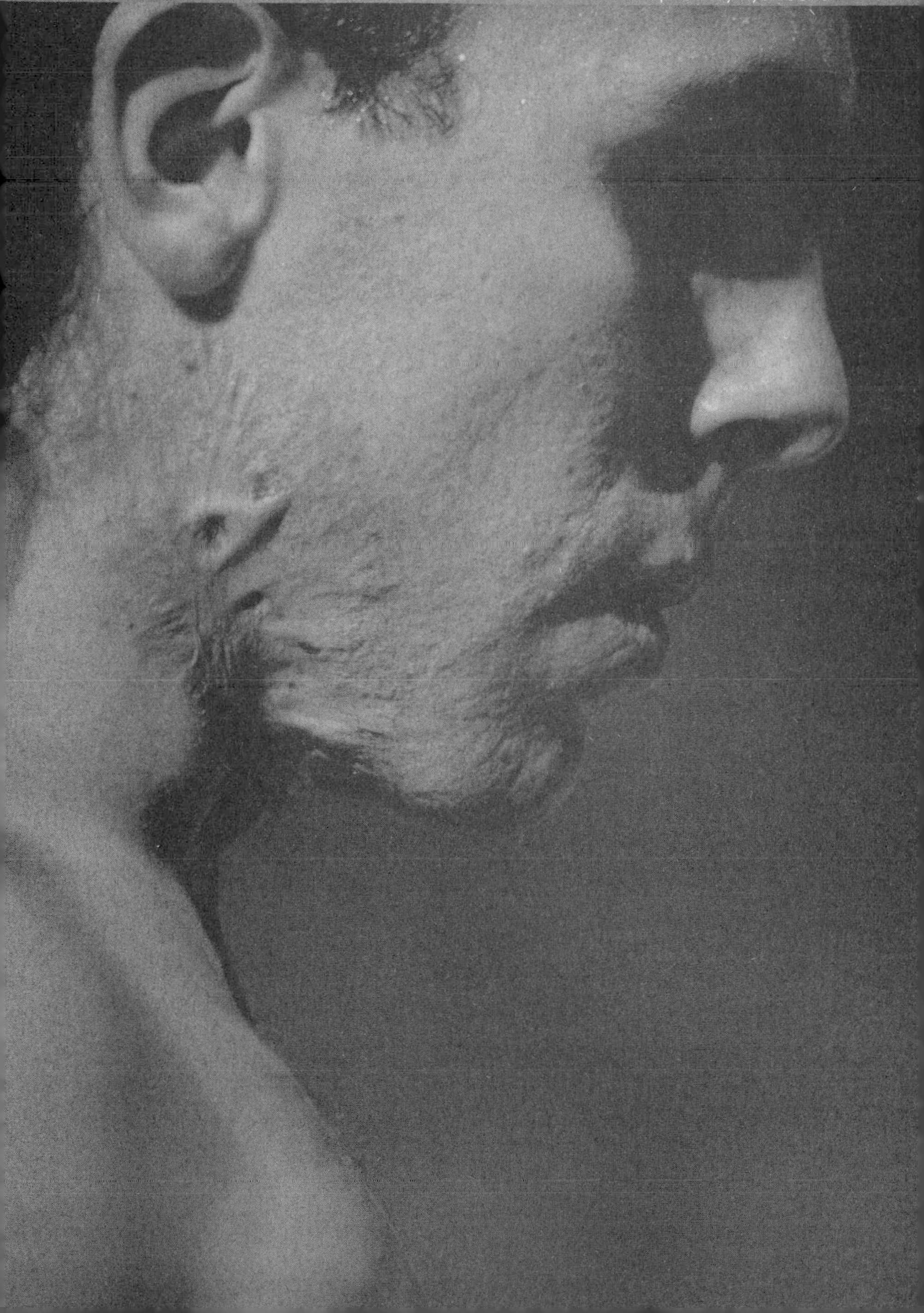

Lionel Andrés Messi

illustration by Kim Sillen Gledhill

BORN:
June 24, 1987
Rosario, Santa Fe
Province, Argentina

HEIGHT: 4'7"

WEIGHT:
98 pounds

POSITION: Striker

TITLE: Golden Boy, by Italian newspaper *Tuttosport*

NICKNAME: it's Leo, La Pulga (The Flea), La Messiah, Submariner (for his propensity to dive)

QUOTE: "There's better to come from me."

TATTOOS: None (that we know of)

VIDEO GAME COVER: Pro-Evolution Soccer 2009

PERSONAL SONG CHANTED BY FANS:
"El Zurdito" (The Little Left Foot)

Most of the crème de la crème world-class soccer players were madly talented prodigies discovered at an early age. But very few of them discovered they had growth hormone deficiency when they were eleven. That's the story of Lionel Messi. Pitted between FC Barcelona and legendary River Plate in his home country of Argentina, he chose sunny Spain because Barcelona agreed to pay the expense of treatment for his condition. And while he didn't grow so big in height, he did in legend, storming onto the world soccer stage like a gaucho magician. At seventeen, he became Barcelona's youngest ever La Liga scorer, and was hailed the next Diego Maradona, by none other than Saint Diego himself.

The story gets dark here. On his international debut, against Hungary, in 2005, Messi threw a vicious elbow, and was shown a red card, ejected in shameful disgrace. Many thought his soccer career might be over, following his emotional, histrionic reaction, which rubbed lots of people in high places the wrong way. But talent won out. And sure enough, when given another chance, Messi became the youngest World Cup scorer in the history of Argentina. And more recently, the small man's larger-than-life display in the European club championship against Manchester United cemented his place as one of the best in the world.

The Flea has time and again mesmerized with his mazy, crazy, wavy gravy runs, where he dribbles through four or five players and then, with the cool of a professional killer, slots the ball home. And that's just what Diego Maradona, the Argentinian coach, hopes to see lots and lots of in South Africa in World Cup 2010, while people endlessly compare Lionel Messi to Diego himself.

Despite a growth-hormone deficiency that earned him the nickname "The Flea," Messi has been hailed as the next Maradona.

RIVALRY &
GRUDGE CO.
PURVEYORS OF
THE FINEST MATCHES
AND DIE-HARD
ANTAGONISM

BRAZIL VS.
ARGENTINA
EDITION

It's the battle of the dances. Samba versus tango. Samba with a freestyle, tango a disciplined force, and when they mix, Kaboom! Brazil has the best player ever: Pelé. So does Argentina: Maradona. And if you want to fight about it, they will. They hate each other.

The Battle of the South Americans has been raging for decades. In a 1946 clash, brutal tackles caused players to fight one another, prompting a pitch invasion by the fans. Mayhem! The countries refused to play each other again. It lasted ten years. Then Brazil bred the One. Pelé led his country to the Promised Land, three World Cup triumphs in twelve years. Argentina was lost in the wilderness.

They waited decades for their Messiah. He was born in an unstable hovel but soon wise men saw that he had many riches in his feet.

But El Diego Maradona was no saint. His playing style was aggressive. His personal life combustible, with nightclubs, cocaine and booze preferred to a quiet night in watching television. And he loathed Pelé.

Feuds never die in soccer. In 2009, Pelé suggested Maradona may not be the best role model for aspiring youth. Maradona's response was thoughtful with nuance: "What do you want me to say? He lost his virginity to a man." Every Brazilian felt the kick in the balls. Brazil salivates at the prospect of nailing Argentina, now coached by El Diego, in the 2010 Finals. South America is not big enough for these two giants. Things are likely to remain ugly, and filled with fabulous insult.

**BRAZIL
vs.
ARGENTINA**

1914
to
forever

Pelé and Maradona—still kicking each others' balls.

Robson de Souza: Robinho

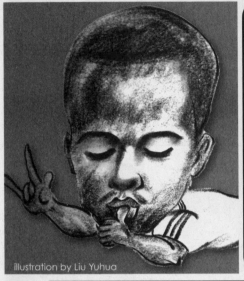

BORN:
Jan. 25, 1984
São Vicente,
São Paulo

HEIGHT: 5'8"

POSITION:
Striker

illustration by Liu Yuhua

NICKNAME: Robinho (the Little Robin); King of the Dribble, King of the Pedalada

SONG: "We've Got Robinho!"

QUOTE: "It is like dribbling without touching the ball. First I balance the body, as if I were dancing the samba. After that I do the move."

QUOTE FROM PELE: "This kid's going to bring us lots of joy."

TV TRIBUTE: The Robinho Stepover on the Brazilian show *Panic on TV*

FAVORITE FOOD: Feijoada

FAVORITE MUSIC: Pagode

CELEBRATION DANCE: Sucking his thumb, a tribute to his son

Every year, hundreds of thousands of little boys are born in Brazil. Genetically, socially and religiously they are built to be soccer players. And they all grow up in the huge shadow of the greatest of them all: Pelé. Since the retirement of this soccer god, it seems like every new genius who comes up through the ranks of Brazilian soccer is called the next Pelé. When Robson de Souza, a descendant of slaves, emerged from Parque Bitaru, one of the nastiest neighborhoods in São Paulo, at the age of nine years old, he scored seventy-four goals in one season. Was he the one to wear the crown?

Robinho was seventeen when he was signed by world famous Santos in 2002, Pelé's old team, and it wasn't long before top clubs all over the world were salivating for his services. But Santos refused to let him go. After much painful courtship, in 2005 Real Madrid finally agreed to a huge dowry, and was able to consummate a deal that brought Robinho to Spain, along with fame and fortune. By 2008, after two league titles, the honeymoon was over; Robinho was granted a divorce and was wooed to the English premiership, where he immediately began a passionate love affair with the Manchester City fans.

Into every life a little rain must fall, and Robinho has had his share of thundershowers. In 2004, his beloved mother Marina de Souza was kidnapped at gunpoint from a party. It was a terrible time for Robinho as rumors swirled that she was dead. But after paying a ransom, he was reunited with her, and no one was hurt. He then bought her an armored car. Through it all, he has been a goal-scoring machine. And he's done it with Brazilian style and grace, with crazy samba stepovers, and cheeky little touches that make the game so beautiful.

So is Robinho the next Pelé? Millions will be waiting to see if he is worthy of the crown in South Africa.

The Little Robin—King of the Dribble

BRAT STATS

Fastest red card to a substitute: Bolivia's Marco Etcheverry, who was sent off after 3 minutes of play as a substitute in the match against Germany on 6/17/94.

Fastest yellow card given to a substitute in finals: Korea Republic's Cha Doo-Ri after 20 seconds in a group match against Poland on 4 June 2002.

Only non-playing reserve players to have been sent off in finals: Yugoslavia's Srečko Katanec on 6/30/90 & Argentina's Claudio Caniggia on 6/12/02.

Fastest sending-off in finals: Uruguay's José Batista, who was sent off in the 56th second of a group match against Scotland on 6/13/86.

Fastest substitution in Finals: Italy's Giuseppe Bergomi replacing Alessandro Nesta in the 4th minute in a First Round match against Austria on 6/23/98.

Fastest yellow card to a player in finals: Sergei Gorlukovich of Russia, who was booked after one minute in a group match against Sweden on 6/24/94.

First player to receive a yellow card: Lovchev of the USSR in the opening match against Mexico on 5/31/70.

photo by Ryu Voelkel

Chile

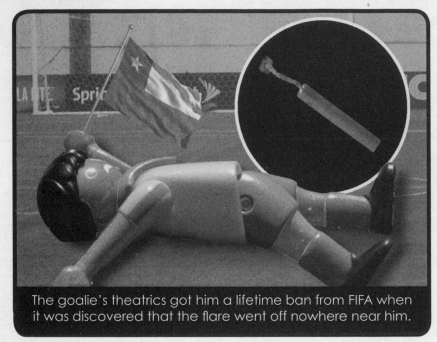

The goalie's theatrics got him a lifetime ban from FIFA when it was discovered that the flare went off nowhere near him.

Hola! We're Chile. Our winds have blown through the World Cup Finals since the tournament's inception in 1930. We are most famous for our disk-shattering battle with the bastard Italians in the most violent World Cup game ever, the Battle of Santiago in 1962. Before the fighting kicked off, we were insulted and abused by the Italian newspapers, determined to claim that wine, women, and *fútbol* were better in the boot of Europe than in the spine of South America. A bloodbath, deeper than the rich flavors of a Chilean *roja*, ensued. Karate kicks, right hooks, and cojones busting boots prompted the army to intervene on the field. We beat them.

Sticking the boot in, that was our style, and things reached a boiling point when the fascist *cabrón* General Pinochet stormed up field and took over the country in a coup. His idea of a game at the

84

national stadium, where we played our soccer matches, was to round up and murder the commies and socialists. All the good players! Our *fútbol* suffered. The Cold War winds blew hard, and the Soviet Union refused to play a World Cup playoff against us, in *el cabrón's* stadium of death. It was the most absurd World Cup game ever. Chile kicked off alone, as the Soviets refused to show, ran the ball down the field, and scored, securing our place in Germany '74. *Que vergüenza*, Pinochet!

In 1989, in a qualifying match against Brazil, our goalkeeper dropped to the turf in agony. A Brazilian *perra* threw a firecracker at him. Our boys refused to play on, hoping FIFA would punish Brazil in the aftermath. But television coverage of the incident betrayed our loco goalie. The flare came nowhere near him. His theatrics got us expelled from the World Cup in 1990 and 1994. He received a lifetime ban from FIFA, and from every bar in Santiago. Lesson One: *Never hire a bad actor as your goalie.*

But that's the old chilly Chile. The current team, under the guidance of former Argentina coach Marcelo Bielsa, plays the most attractive soccer in South America. We're all about attacking wing play, and a fast-passing game. Defenses have been eaten up, and washed down with a vintage *fútbol* flavor. It's wonderful to see the wing game being embraced again. Amigos, we will be moving on from *vino* to champagne in South Africa.

CHILE FACTS

Weather: Quite chilly in the winter
Population: 16 million
Capital: Santiago
Calling code: 56
Language: Spanish
Independence achieved:
1810, from Spain
Mountains: The Andes
National slogan: By Right or by Might

UNDERDOGS: CAMEROON

Italy '90

Cameroon. Who? Argentina was the first big heads to have their noses bloodied by the "Indomitable Lions" during the 1990 Finals in Italy. Cameroon beat them 1-0 in the opening game, and with nine men.

The heat of Africa's fiercest roar came from Roger Milla, an aging striker who had been included in the squad at the insistence of Cameroon's president. He proved that goal-scoring beauty did not belong exclusively to the young. His goals against Romania and Colombia were crackers. His celebratory dance at the corner flag became a sensation. In public parks and on the streets, wherever soccer was played, kids were doing the Roger Milla shuffle. Fast, proud, and with a killer instinct for goal, this lion's bite struck fear into every soccer powerhouse.

The English were next: in the quarterfinal. Trembling English hands grasped cups of tea before the match. Cameroon was now the pride of the tournament. Their fabulous flying soccer mane was a riot of color and beauty. The gold and green of their uniforms blended with the grasslands of the field. The scent of World Cup glory was now in the air. Only the flag of the English stood in the way.

England scored, Cameroon tied, and then scored a goal of sublime beauty to lead. Eight minutes remained. The semifinal beckoned. The British Empire was about to be sent home. But the referee had other ideas and England was sent victorious by two late penalty kicks. Beauty was slain by beastly rules. But the African underdog had gone from bark to bite.

The question is, which underdog will rear their heads and roar in 2010?

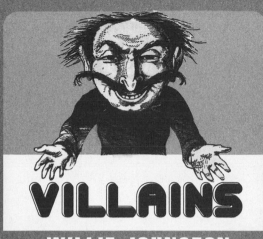

VILLAINS

VIOLENCE

ALCOHOL

DRUGS

WILLIE JOHNSTON

Willie Johnston was dead fast playing down the wing. Being Scottish, he grew up drinking lots of tea. Ten cups a day was normal. You got the impression that Johnston didn't sleep. He was included in Scotland's drunken 1978 squad for Argentina. After the first game, he was ordered to pee in a cup. After filtration for alcohol and tea, the cloudy specimen revealed a banned stimulant. Willie Johnston became the first player in World Cup history to be sent home in disgrace for drug abuse. He left Argentina at gunpoint. His family suffered verbal abuse after his return to Scotland, the land of tea, whisky and silly monsters.

Johnston's nickname was Bud, a rather unfortunate moniker for a man with a dope record. Once, before taking a corner kick, he took a big Scottish swig from a fan's can of beer. He was sent off over twenty times in his career. An opponent needed the kiss of life after Bud stamped on his neck during a televised game. In retirement, he refused to follow the traditional path open to soccer players; management, coaching, punditry. He went to work in a bar. Willie Johnston was one of Scotland's greatest hard drinking-players.

DEATH

VIOLENCE

ALCOHOL

DRUGS

MADNESS

NUDITY

INSULT

TERRORISM

The World Cup Through Tellys
by Alan Black

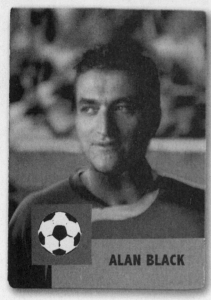

ALAN BLACK

invited me to watch the game on his new color TV. With him was Mr. Aitken, his neighbor, the Scottish version of a suicide bomber. He couldn't wait to explode.

Mr. Elliott's son was my pal. We said nothing. We watched. We were nine. Mr. Aitken was on his third can of strong lager ten minutes into the game. The blue can of beer had a scantily clad girl pictured on it. Mr Aitken's hand was stroking her when Scotland had possession, or gripping her roughly when Zaire pushed up into Scotland's half. His red nose sprouted blue when Scotland had a scoring chance, and popped purple when Zaire threatened. Low bursts of "shites" and "f***" wobbled out from behind his yellow teeth. Finally, Scotland scored. Mr. Aitken flew up like a trebuchet's fireball and landed on top of Mr. Elliott's color TV. The scantily clad girl on the side of the beer

Color. Life had been in black and white up until Scotland played Zaire in the Finals of 1974. The qualifying games were watched in my house in gray, slated tones against teams like Czechoslovakia. The Communist Eastern Bloc was not too colorful, so nothing was missed. But Zaire was from Africa. They were a hot spread. Their yellow shirts were doomed in black and white. So Mr. Elliott

can stared up from the green carpet, bleak Scottish lager leaking from her spout. An orange lager-fall poured down the screen of Mr. Elliott's color TV, making the Zaire shirts look zany. Mr. Elliott said to Mr. Aitken—*You've ruined my bloody telly!* Mr. Aitken left to watch the rest of the game in his house, alone, on his black-and-white.

During the Finals, eight years later, in a hotel bar in Spain, a tumbling beer mug flew over my head, and crash-landed on the TV screen. A Spanish waiter had an Irishman by the throat. It looked like rain on the plain Spanish telly. The box blinked in disbelief at the insult, and the score—Northern Ireland 1, Spain 0. The following day, the telly was gone. The manager told me it was broken but I imagined he removed it to save his bar from being trashed during the later stages of the tournament. The World Cup, he said, *Ya que?*

Mexico '86 was viewed on a portable 13-inch color. This was around the time

Scottish soccer was shrinking as a threat to others. Our players were getting smaller as the rest of the world was getting bigger. We continued to live on a diet of potato chips and cigarettes while nations previously inferior to us invested in vegetables, and grew. By the time the big-screen TV arrived in the nineties, Scotland had shrunk to a minor pixel, and lost to countries that had only just discovered electricity.

In 2002, I watched the Asian World Cup in a Korean-owned Scottish theme bar, where I worked as a bartender. Koreans are much like the Scots. They quickly change channels from friendliness to aggression depending on the score. They like to drink, smoke and curse, and hate a bigger enemy. Their culture was trampled upon, and they love football. Korea is the Scotland of Asia, except Korea wins.

South Korea played Italy in the quarterfinal, and won the game with a golden goal. In front of a packed and shocked room, the bar owner exploded at the big-screen TV he had rented, lifted it off the table, and held it aloft like an Asian Incredible Hulk. His primal scream melted the rocks in the glasses, before the TV fell on top of him. It was a moment of high definition: the glory of the World Cup.

Alan Black All-Time World Cup XI

Ronnie Hellström

John Blackley

Giacinto Facchetti

Franco Baresi

Claudio Gentile

Graeme Souness

Diego Maradona

Frank Rijkaard

Pak Doo-Ik

Grzegorz Lato

Johan Neeskens

HISTORY OF THE BALLS

The leather lace-up, used in the 1930 World Cup

Once the ham had been eaten with the eggs, after breakfast, the pig's bladder was blown up and booted around. Problem was, no one could tell where it was likely to fly, or bounce. And soon enough, it would burst with a dying squeal. Soccer was a game of farce. Someone had to fix it. Mr Goodyear did. He invented the vulcanized rubber ball in 1836. Players could now concentrate on their skills.

The ball's role in the game goes far. Its history stretches across panels of suspicion and style, luck and blame. The 1930 World Cup Final between rivals Argentina and Uruguay was played with two balls. Mistrust between the two nations was normal. Each believed that they should supply the ball for the Final, as the other was likely to fix it in their favor. How to prejudice a soccer ball was never scientifically explained. Who needed Einstein to explain how cheats found a way? It was agreed Argentina would provide the ball for the first half, Uruguay the second. Predictably, Argentina was up 2-1 at half-time. At full-time, the result was 4-2 to Uruguay. They carried the trophy and their magic ball home.

The leather ball with laces replaced Goodyear's rubber but it was hardly an improvement. On a rainy day, it was as heavy as a sack of potatoes. Heading destroyed necks and caused low IQs in soccer players. Taking it in the groin required a new set of family jewels. Coming to the rescue was Adidas. The company commenced making balls in 1963, and by 1970, they had the contract with FIFA cemented. The glory age of the ball began.

Mexico '70 introduced the ball as an icon, the classic "Telstar." Using the Buckminster Fuller design, the Buckyball was formed around a pagan patchwork of hexagons and pentagons, stitched perfectly to form an almost perfect sphere. The black panels helped players see the ball better, and aided television viewing in the age of black and white. The ball speed was rapidly increased due to improved materials and the aerodynamic design. Some of the stunning goals of Mexico '70, including the Brazilian Carlos Alberto's thunder strike in the Final, could not have occurred with older balls.

The '70 "Telstar"

From then on, each World Cup has had a signature ball. The classic "Tango" appeared in 1978 and helped Argentina dance to glory. By 1982 in Spain, the Tango had evolved to waterproof seams. Not that it was needed in Iberia, but across the wet soccer world it revolutionized the game for players used to kicking soggy bricks. The "Azteca" was rolled out in Mexico '86 and was the first synthetic model. Throughout the nineties further innovations emerged; polyethylene foam under the ball's surface heralded a new age of control for players, rapidly increasing the velocity of the ball, and making goalkeepers' lives more difficult. Just what they needed.

The ball is the ghost in football. It spooks and astonishes us. And when the game is over, it lies forgotten on the field, as the mortals sing and dance or weep and slump. And then to kick off again, to capture us.

The '82 "Tango"

photo by Ryu Voelkel

Tsubasa's death-defying heroics in stopping a school bus with just a soccer ball made him a sensation with kids.

Captain Tsubasa! Thank him, Sensei, for Japanese *sakkaa*. Before our *manga* soccer hero, Captain Tsubasa, came along in the eighties, the Japanese game was dominated by the slave driver bosses. Players stripped for the company team, having to work in the plant by day, and play football for the boss on weekends. Soon, our quality players were climbing gangplanks, and sailing off to countries that would pay them. *Konaro!*

Our hero, Captain Tsubasa, taught us how to fight back. He made the *sakkaa* ball our friend. As a one-year-old, Tsubasa was saved from death from an oncoming bus, by using his ball as a buffer to deflect the blow. What a play! Nothing could kill him. He was the miracle boy born to play *sakkaa*. We wanted to be like Tsubasa; we wanted glory. So we gathered up our baseball bats and threw them at our parents. "I don't want that Yankee crap. I want a *sakkaa* ball, *Okasan!*" Fifteen years after Tsubasa's debut, and his rise to *sakkaa's* lofty heights, Japan qualified for its first World Cup Finals, hosted the tournament four years later, and became an Asian soccer powerhouse. *Banzai!*

Our Blue Samurai are approaching South Africa with more determination than ever. Coach Takeshi Okada has drilled into our team the dynamo of discipline and hard work. Our midfield moves the ball around with the swiftness of the wind, and our attack is as lethal as a sword swiping the heads of defenders. Admittedly, and with shame on them and their families, the team has struggled in the past with goal scoring. To compete against the world's heavyweight teams, we will need to find a new hybrid fuel ratio of goals to games. The players need to channel their inner Captain Tsubasa, and perform the miracle moves for Nippon. World, don't be shocked if we pull off some big surprises in South Africa. The land of the rising sun will have its day. And Captain Tsubasa will rule *sakkaa*.

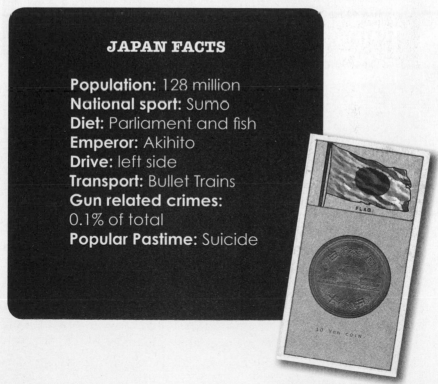

JAPAN FACTS

Population: 128 million
National sport: Sumo
Diet: Parliament and fish
Emperor: Akihito
Drive: left side
Transport: Bullet Trains
Gun related crimes: 0.1% of total
Popular Pastime: Suicide

WORLD CUP TRIVIA

Get it right!

1.) At 17 years and 239 days, who is the youngest player to score a goal in the tournament?

A) Pelé
B) Ronaldo
C) Ronaldinho
D) Someone who isn't Brazilian

2.) At 42 years and 39 days, who is the oldest player to score a goal?

A) Paolo Maldini
B) Roger Milla
C) Socrates
D) Plato

3.) At 17 years and 358 days, who is the youngest player to be sent off?

A) Wayne Rooney
B) Norman Whiteside
C) Rigoberto Song
D) Luca Brazzi

4.) Who saved the most penalty kicks (2) in the same Finals?

A) Dino Zoff
B) Brad Friedel
C) Jan Tomaszewski
D) Pelé

5.) Who was the only player to win three World Cups?

A) Giuseppe Meazza
B) Vava
C) Cafu
D) Pelé

6.) Who scored the most goals (5) in a Finals match?

A) Gerd Müller
B) Juste Fontaine
C) Oleg Salenko
D) Friedrich Nietzsche

7.) Who was the only player to score for both teams in a match?

A) Andrés Escobar
B) Ernie Brandts
C) Jairzinho
D) Niccolo Machiavelli

8.) Who has the longest surname?

A) Jan Venegoor of Hossollink
B) Ricardo Izecsondosantosleite
C) Lefter Kucukandonyadis
D) Miroslav van Supercalifragilisticexpialidocious

9.) Which goalkeeper conceded the most goals (16) in one Finals?

A) Jorge Campos
B) Yung Hong Duk
C) Alan Rough
D) Alexander Vakkemoff

10.) Who are the only championship players to win a championship as coaches?

A) Mario Zagalo
B) Aimé Jacquet
C) Franz Beckenbauer
D) Nelson Mandela

Player Profile:
Arjen Robben

illustration by Liu Yuhua

BORN:
January 23, 1984
Bedum, Groningen,
Netherlands

POSITION: Winger

HEIGHT: 5' 11½"

NICKNAME: The Flying Dutchman; Batman and Robben (with Mateja Kežman)

QUOTE: "I put my brains in neutral and told myself, 'I will make it.'"

AGENT: Hans Robben, his dad

HOBBY: Chess

PERSONAL SONG CHANTED BY FANS:
"I told my mate the other day
That I have found the white Pelé.
My mate said, who, who is it, then?
I told him that it was Arjen Robben."

The Sir Stanley Matthews move, the scissors, double scissors, the Rivelino, the Elastico, and the Cruyff. These are all moves mastered by the new Dutch master, Arjen Robben. He learned them all at Coerver's school of football skills as a little Dutch boy hanging around the dikes. His whippet quickness and fearless desire pegged him as a treasure. Legendary Dutch club PSV Eindhoven had him

Robben has become infamous for his Oscar-worthy dives.

on display at the ripe old age of sixteen. Chelsea was next to show the diamond, and back-to-back Premier League championships followed. Real Madrid stole him, and his dazzling trickery helped the Royalists to another crown.

The dark spot in Robben's dazzle is his reputation as a world-class diver with Daniel Day-Lewis–caliber performances. He first came to prominence as a "submariner" against Portugal in Euro 2004 followed by an incident that made him a laughingstock. Liverpool goalkeeper Pepe Reina lightly touched Robben on the cheek, and he fell like he had been shot by a semiautomatic weapon. Later, Reina said, "He deserved an Oscar."

Robben first pulled on the historic Orange of Holland at the tender age of twenty, and scored the winning goal against Serbia and Montenegro in World Cup 2006. Championships seem to follow Robben everywhere he goes. Perhaps in the shadow of Robben Island, apartheid's infamous prison, Arjen will help his team burrow their way to the Final.

RIVALRY &
GRUDGE CO.
PURVEYORS OF
THE FINEST MATCHES
AND DIE-HARD
ANTAGONISM

HOLLAND VS.
GERMANY
EDITION

War. What is it good for? Absolutely soccer. These might be the lyrics of a tribute song to the bitter rivalry between these soccer powers. A fertile harvest of hatred has gathered since the Germans marched into Rotterdam in 1940.

Look at the charge sheet. At the end of their match up at Euro '88, Ronald Koeman, the Dutch defender, simulated an ass-wipe with a defeated German shirt. The Dutch fans sang, "In 1940 they came. In 1988 we came." Two years later, at the World Cup in Italy, Dutch ace Frank Rijkaard spat on German striker Rudi Völler. Red card for Frank, and Völler! In 2006, months before the Finals in Germany, a Dutch factory spat out replica Nazi-style plastic helmets emblazoned in Dutch orange with the ironic slogan, *Attack Netherlands!* When the Dutch government objected to the insensitivity toward their larger neighbor, every man, woman and child in Holland placed an order. The German response to Holland's elimination from the tournament was to construct a road sign on the Autobahn. It read, "Holland, Next Exit."

In a nod to the powers of the stereotype, the Dutch have clogs, windmills, pot cafés, bicycles, and dikes. The Germans have boots, castles, beer gardens, Porsches and musclemen. Neither the twain shall meet. Their rivalry is one of the best. Let's hope in the land of the Dutch Boers, they meet each other on the great trek to the Final.

**HOLLAND
vs.
GERMANY**

1940
to
today

Dutch defender Ronald Koeman provoked a scandal by wiping his ass with German player Olaf Thon's shirt.

VILLAINS

AUSTRIA AND WEST GERMANY

INSULT

The most disgraceful match played in World Cup history was between Germany and old friend Austria in Gijón, Spain, in 1982. Like the shameless cowards they were, they concocted a scheme ensuring both of them would qualify at rival Algeria's expense. The German speakers passed the ball amongst themselves for seventy-nine minutes, knowing that Germany's eleventh-minute goal ensured that both would qualify for the second round of the tournament. Sportscasters gave up commentating on the game. The crowd booed and left the stadium. After the Finals, FIFA was forced to change the rules, demanding that the final matchups in the first round be played contemporaneously. The game came to be known as the Shame of Gijón, and will never be forgotten in Algeria. But karma being what it is, Italy defeated West Germany in the Final, preventing a stain being engraved on the trophy.

DEATH VIOLENCE ALCOHOL DRUGS MADNESS NUDITY INSULT TERRORISM

photo by Ryu Voelkel

Michael Ballack

BORN:
September 26, 1976

HEIGHT: 6'2"

WEIGHT: 176 pounds

POSITION: Midfield

NICKNAME: Kleine Kaiser (Little Kaiser), Balla

QUOTE:
"We have to be very aggressive, to go to the limit of what's legal."

PET: Sancho, the dog

FAVORITE COMIC: Werner

FAVORITE ACTOR: Al Pacino

FAVORITE DESIGNERS: Dolce & Gabbana, Donna Karan and Gucci

FAVORITE PERFUME: Romance

PERSONAL SONG CHANTED BY FANS:
(to the tune of "99 Balloons") "99 balloons *und* strudel, Ballack loves to comb his poodle, How are you in the Chelsea side, when all your shots go ten yards wide?"

Seven years old. That's how old he was when Michael Ballack's parents put him on the train to become a fußball player. German soccer meisters are supposed to be cerebral, elegant, ruthless, technically brilliant, coldbloodedly efficient and just brutal enough to win the world championship. Michael Ballack seemed almost destined to become the latest torch holder in a long line of German soccer legends, given the name of his first club. BSG Motor Karl-Marx-Stadt. That combination of fast-running motor and intellectual precision have helped Ballack on his slow and steady climb from small fish Kaiserslautern to big fish Bayern München to gigantic killer whale Chelsea. Along the way he was named German soccer player of the year three times, European midfielder of the year, and one of FIFA's Hundred Greatest Living Players.

As stratospheric as his career has been, Ballack has the unfortunate distinction of being runner-up for three major championships in a season. Not once, but twice, with Bayern Leverkusen (dubbed the "Horrible Treble" in the German press), and Chelsea. But he has also proven time and again that when his team needs a big tackle, a perfectly weighted pass, or a thunderous free kick, the Kleine Kaiser, or Little Kaiser (after Franz Beckenbauer, the original Kaiser), finds a way to get it done. And that's just what he hopes to do in South Africa in 2010.

Ballack's love of labels has earned him something of a fashion-plate reputation.

SEX AND SUCCER, SOCCER AND SEX

There's something about soccer that seems to bring out the animal in people. The fanatical excitement, the beat of the drums, all those balls; it just seems to get the juices flowing. The history of the World Cup has been splattered with angry wives, fishy mistresses, and team officials trying to keep their players' libidos under control.

Traditionally, there has been the idea that abstinence makes the team grow stronger. But there is just as long a tradition of the best and brightest soccer players from all over the world being randy shaggers, then going out and stroking the ball about, with calm yet energetic brilliance. Only time will tell whether celibacy or carousing will win the World Cup in South Africa in 2010.

illustration by Liu Yuhua

HEY, RONALDO, TAKE A WALK THE WILD SIDE

Did he or didn't he? Was he a she or wasn't he? These are just some of the questions that came up when Brazil's World Cup hero, Ronaldo, hired three ladies of the evening. But when he brought them back to his hotel room, he was in for a big surprise. Actually, three big surprises — they were dudes. Depending on whom you believe, they tried to extort the World Cup winner, or he tried it on and refused to pay. He told police he was having psychological problems due to an injury. Aren't we all?

NO SEX FOR YOU!

Costa Rican soccer players were overjoyed when they qualified for World Cup 2006 in Germany. Imagine how they, their wives and their mistresses felt, when they were informed by Costa Rican officials that they would have to give up sex. "We are professionals and we know that this is part of the sacrifice we have to make. At the World Cup we have to abstain," José Francisco Porras, the team goalkeeper, is reported to have said. They finished the first group stage with zero points.

MAD DOG ROONEY – A MAN OF THE PEOPLE

World Cup star Wayne Rooney, who makes upward of $40 million a year, was preparing for a national team appearance at a whorehouse in the seedy underbelly of Liverpool, according to tabloid sensation. An astonished fellow reveler—who asked Wayne, "What are YOU doing here?"— recognized him. Mr. Rooney never missed a beat: "Same as you, la'." The newspaper reported he paid $90 for sex, to a booming granny affectionately nicknamed "Auld Slapper" by fellow sex workers. Another industrial sex technician claimed Rooney paid her $260 for a romp in the bathroom of a filthy flat, and left her a beautiful love note: "To Charlotte, I shagged U on 28 Dec, loads of love, Wayne Rooney."

SEX AND SOUTH AFRICA

The foreplay leading up to World Cup 2010 has been hot and heavy when it comes to sex for money. Many are calling for a tight fist to crack down on ladies of the evening. Michael Sutcliffe, Durban's city manager, argues that it should be a crime, and soccer fanatics who pay for it should be criminals. Parliament Member George Lekgetho, on the other hand, believes South Africa should open her arms as well as her legs to the world in 2010. This is an important part of being a good host. According to him, "It is one of the things that would make the World Cup a success." Whether you're for it or against it, one thing is for sure. There is plenty of sex coming to South Africa at World Cup 2010.

illustration by Liu Yuhua

THE HOOLIES

The United Nations of Hooligans...
The Hoolie having his breakfast

Hey! Don't forget us! You can't have a World Cup without us hooligans. How would the bar owners of South Africa make any money if it wasn't for us filling their tills with our hard-earned cash? And how would the nice policeman be able to afford a decent vacation for his family without that valuable overtime money he earns, keeping us hooligans apart? Not a lot of people give us credit for supporting police families. And who would sing in the stadiums in South Africa if we were not invited to the biggest show on earth? The rich people sitting on their golden hinds? Don't make me laugh. It's we who sing, we hooligans, the choir of soccer.

So pull out the old suitcase and start packing — passport, rands, the Consulate's number, knives, suntan lotion, scarf, aspirin, and a guidebook to the taverns of South Africa.

Look over there. It's the English boys, many from small towns in darkest England, where nothing ever happens but rain and pain. Eng-a-land! The dragon's breath, cor blimey, give that boy some chewing gum. They're not much for the personal hygiene, some of these provincials, but the top boys from the city know the value of a good toothbrush, a clean shave and fine sneakers. Forty years is a long time to wait for an English hand on the World Cup trophy, and many of these boys saw their fathers die, without seeing England prevail. How long can they wait?

Look up! What's that flying in the sky? Is it a bird? Is it a plane? No, it's the Serbian hooligans firing flares. These comrades are always looking to settle a few historic scores, and it should be a nice little rematch when they come up against Germany in the Finals.

Speaking of horrible history, there are some unusual mobs packing their aftershave for a visit to South Africa. Rumor has it that the North Koreans are capable of organizing a surprise attack at any time, especially if they end up meeting their wealthy southern brothers in the kebab shop after the game. And sources in the wide world of hoolies suggest the Irish mobs are planning on showing up even though they are not in the tournament. They're looking for some geezer called Henry even though their best shot might be chasing a few frogs out on the safari.

With the World Cup way down south this time round, you might get some of those Argentine barra bravas making the trip across the big wide sea, following the Maradona God, ready to pelt the nice Brazilians with more venom than a bucket of snakes on a picnic. And that's how they'll bite you, the boys from the barrios, right in the neck. They're not so much into dancing as into stomping, and it's been a while since the trophy has been on display in Buenos Aires. When Saint Diego makes the call for the bravas to follow, expect bigger crowds than Jesus pulled when he was touring the hotspots.

But don't think we Northern Hemisphere hoolies don't know what kind of trouble you local lads are capable of. We hear Nigeria likes to stick the boot in, and Ivory Coast can whip it up. And as for you, South Africa, you've got your own fighters. They tell us your army is preparing for any eventuality, with tanks, planes, guns, and spies ready to infiltrate the mobs. We've seen it all before. Just make sure the beer is warm, the streets can be used for peeing, and a kebab can be had at 3 in the morning. Then all should be quiet on the southern front.

So, South Africa, are you ready for an invasion? We hoolies want to come, and join in the party on Table Top Mountain. So it's down the travel agent to get the tickets, and…Wait a minute….How many hours is the plane ride? You must be joking. We're scared of flying. Maybe we hoolies will just stay at home, with our mums, and watch it on the telly.

A common sighting of the hooligan in his natural habitat.

photo by Ryu Voelkel

MORE BRAT STATS

Only player to have played in Final for two different countries: Luis Monti, who played for Argentina in the 1930 Final and for Italy in the 1934 Final.

Most headed goals by a player in the same Finals: 5 goals, by Miroslav Klose of Germany in the 2002 Finals.

Most goals by a player in Finals in aggregate: 15 goals, by Ronaldo of Brazil in the Finals of 1998, 2002 & 2006.

Most goals conceded by a goalkeeper in the same Finals: 16 goals, by Korean goalkeeper Yung Hong Duk in two 1954 Finals matches.

Only player to have scored in Finals for two different countries: Robert Prosinečki, who scored for Yugoslavia in 1990 and for Croatia in 1998.

Most goals by a player in a Finals match: 5 goals, by Russia's Oleg Salenko against Cameroon on 6/28/94.

Youngest champion player: Brazil's Pelé, who was 17 years old when he played in the 1958 Final.

Oldest champion player: Dino Zoff, the goalkeeper & captain of Italy, who was 40 when he played in the 1982 Final.

Worst Attended Game: 300, Romania & Peru in Montevideo on 7/14/1930

Best Attended Game: 199,850 Brazil & Uruguay in Rio de Janeiro on 7/16/1950

Most Finals matches by a goalkeeper without conceding a goal: 10 matches by Peter Shilton of England from 1982 to 1990.

Longest scoreless streak by a goalkeeper: 518 minutes, by Walter Zenga of Italy in the 1986 & 1990 finals.

Best Gift for Goal Scored: United Arab Emirates. In 1990 goal scorers received a Rolls Royce for every goal they scored!

Worst Refereeing: English referee Graham Poll gave out three yellow cards to Josip Šimunić in the Australia versus Croatia game, 2006.

VILLAINS

TERRORISM

MADNESS

AL-QAEDA TERRORISTS

Before the 2006 World Cup Finals in Germany, an Al-Qaeda offshoot in Saudi Arabia issued a *fatwa* against modern soccer. The madmen demanded that the rules of the game be changed to fit their bizarre game plan. Players were instructed not to wear uniforms but to play in pajamas, and to abandon celebrations of goals. The length of each half was to be shortened, as the regulation forty-five minutes was a Zionist conspiracy to enslave the Muslim world. The terrorist nutters had some support outside of their cave for abandoning the need for referees. And countries on the end of frequent heavy defeats supported the *fatwa's* edict of not keeping score, as counting goals was an infidel's plot to enforce Western accountancy, and its ennui, on the Islamic world. The Al-Qaeda squad would be made up of ten *jihadis* with no substitutes allowed. And it went without saying that women should never be allowed to kick balls, although many would like to.

DEATH   VIOLENCE   ALCOHOL   DRUGS   MADNESS   NUDITY   INSULT   TERRORISM

RIVALRY & GRUDGE CO.
PURVEYORS OF
THE FINEST MATCHES
AND DIE-HARD
ANTAGONISM

¡Viva el Salvador!

Ole Honduras!

EL SALVADOR VS.
HONDURAS
EDITION

When these two postage stamp countries decided to lick each other after a World Cup qualifying game, the sticky mess was bloody. The Football War kicked off after El Salvador eliminated Honduras in a playoff battle for a place in Mexico '70. The teams met in two games before a fateful playoff; both matches were marred by crowd trouble and police violence. Incendiary press attacks in both countries stoked the hatreds, and decades-old political and social tensions fueled the flames. The playoff pulled the trigger, 2,000 civilians died, and 300,000 people were displaced before the Organization of American States, acting as referee, blew time on a nasty four-day war. The wounds never healed.

The playoff game took place in Mexico City, and was tied at 2-2, forcing extra time. The demented game swung back and forth until El Salvador's Pipo Rodriguez slid home the winner, securing his place at El Salvador's top table. Grainy black-and-white film of the match shows Rodriguez being mobbed by photographers, the flashbulbs going off like bombs, a foreshadowing of the explosions that were to fall from the sky a mere two weeks later. There is no better example of soccer's dangerous cannon than the Football War. And it's not likely to be the last time war breaks out after a final whistle.

EL SALVADOR VS. HONDURAS

The Soccer War

The crowd's aggression and police violence defined the playoff game in Mexico City. The unrest was a harbinger of the bloody political conflagration that was to follow between El Salvador and Honduras.

Country Profile:
Australia

G'day, mate. The Socceroos are stormin' up a ripper. For too long, we Aussies did not have a fair shake of the sauce bottle. But World Cup 2006 changed all that. Unlucky and robbed are the words that spring to mind, the Italians stealing our glory in the Round of 16. But not to worry, there's plenty of lolly to go around. Australia is planning to have more than a Captain Cook at the old World Cup next year; we're plotting to stuff it in the pouch and bounce the trophy all the way back to Oz. Fair dinkim, mate.

For a long time, no one cared about soccer Down Under. We have our cricket and our rugby and our own Rules Footie. The rest of the world can go to hell. But airplanes came along and soccer balls were packed into the bags of new immigrants arriving from Europe. Most of them came with a conviction not for stealing sheep but for that old game soccer. So, after a few generations of playing out in the Never Never, we wanted to be part of the big rip snorter party, the World Cup. Results were patchy for a while, things needed time to grow, and then around the turn of the century things began to bloom on the old gum tree, mate. A bunch of quality players were ready for pickings, the likes of Kewell, Viduka, Neill and Cahill, all good spunk. They pulled on the colors and showed the world that Oz had the ham and eggs for the beautiful game.

Thousands of Bruces and Sheilas are likely to pull the strides on and head to South Africa in the winter. There's just one dream that our fans wish to have—a matchup against the Poms. Beating the English at their game would be the highlight of our sporting century. Call it the revenge of the villains. Back to bite the Poms right in the goolies. Ripper! So, South Africa—open up the billabongs, and pour the amber fluid into the billys; there's some thirsty Aussies coming over for a party, mate.

AUSTRALIA FACTS

Population: 58.6 million kangaroos
Others: 21 million homo-sapiens, 5 million boomerangs
Currency: Beer
Government: Commonwealth democracy
Head of State: Lizzie in London
Drive: Hard on the left
National anthem: "Waltzing Matilda"

Player Profile:
Lucas Neill

illustration by Liu Yuhua

Born:
March 9, 1978
Sydney, Australia

Height: 6'1"

Position: Defender

NICKNAME: The Rock

YOUTUBE MOVIE: *World Cup Hottie*

QUOTE: "It's a boyhood dream...We're going to get the chance to go over and create even more history in South Africa."

FAVORITE FOODS: Minties, Twisties, meat pies

TRAINING TECHNIQUE: To become more ambidextrous, trained with right boot off to become better with left

NEWEST HONOR: Bachelor of the Year

FAVORITE HOLIDAY DESTINATION: Las Vegas

The Rock was born Down Under, but he got at least part of his stones from his Irish dad, The Rock, Sr., who was an extremely serious, and equally rugged, player.

Neill is the second youngest player ever to compete for Australia, first becoming a Socceroo at the age of seventeen years against Saudi Arabia. And he has been part of the spinal column of the national team ever since. In 2000, he became an Olyroo, the Australian Olympic team. In November 2005, in a balls-out qualifier against Uruguay, he scored his second penalty, and was named Man of the Match, kangaroo-hopping the Australians into World Cup 2006 after a nail-biting, pulse-pounding, sphincter-clenching campaign. In October 2006, he had the great honor to be named Socceroo captain. He led the Socceroos to a historic, unprecedented second consecutive World Cup qualification in South Africa.

The Rock is known far and wide for being a granite-hard, take-no-prisoners-and-leave-them-bowed-and-bloodied defender, who also happens to have some crazy attacking skills, among them being a vicious header of the ball. In fact Neill is so hard he became a marked man after his legendary tackle on Liverpool star Jamie Carragher. Apparently, a group of Carragher's teammates were ready to assault The Rock, but Carragher refused to give the go-ahead. The Rock's the kind of guy you love to hate. Except if he's on your team. Then you just love him.

Just don't call him cuddly.

SUMMER OF 1990
by Po Bronson

PO BRONSON

I played in college for Stanford, but somewhere along the line I lost my joy. An athlete's senior season is supposed to be his shining moment. Instead, I never showed up to practice — and couldn't explain to anyone why. That was 1985.

I didn't strap on cleats for four years, when I found myself playing pickup Saturday mornings at the Polo Fields in Golden Gate Park with about twenty internationals—a mix of older Europeans, flamboyant South Americans, and hard-running Africans. This game had been going on, continuously, since the 1970s. Each

year, a few new players met the standard, and a few dropped away. Almost all the players were uncoachable—while they'd all spent a half decade on city club teams, they'd been all booted off for being too selfish and too spontaneous. They loved the nutmeg too much.

Strangely, they never bothered to learn one another's names. Instead, they called one another by the name of their country. Except for the Africans, who were just called, "Africa," and except for me: nobody knew what to make of me. To them, I did not play like an American.

I didn't tell my family I was playing. It was too hard to admit to my father that I was back on the field—not semipro, not even on a club team, but rather just on a patch of grass, without jerseys, with a bunch of rejects, skilled as they might be.

The summer of 1990, the opener of the World Cup matched the defending champion, Argentina, against Cameroon—who was widely expected to lose. The day before, we enacted our own mock opener in Golden Gate Park—the South Americans wanted to take on The World. I was thrown together with the Africans. Joey announced he was from Cameroon, which entitled him to be our captain. We fought honorably in defeat, in a match that lasted 2.5 hours.

After the game, Joey gave me the highest compliment: "You play like an African, my friend." I dropped the name of Tony Igwe, one of the most famous Nigerian players. Igwe had captained the Nigerian Olympic team in 1968, and even guarded Pelé in an exhibition game in Lagos in 1972 when Nigeria played Santos. He was one of my coaches at Stanford. To Joey, this explained everything. He turned to the other Africans and pronounced me an honorary African.

The next morning, at Joey's cramped apartment, we all watched as his country shocked the world, defeating Maradona's team 1-nil

despite losing two players on red cards. Later that week, we watched as thirty-eight-year-old substitute Roger Milla came to the rescue, netting two to beat favored Romania and putting Cameroon's Indomitable Lions through into the Round of 16.

That Saturday in Golden Gate Park, it was Africa's turn to take on The World. Joey wore his green Cameroon jersey. The South Americans felt I should play for them, The World. Joey refused, explaining my honorary status. Fueled by pride over his nation's amazing ride, Joey was unstoppable. Repeatedly, he encouraged us by calling out "African style!" which meant keeping the ball on the ground and out of the air. For once, unselfish play was the rule, rather than the exception. We always played until one team quit, and pride didn't break easily—it was three hours before The World accepted they'd never catch up. By then, the score was 15-3.

No African team had ever made the World Cup quarterfinals, but everyone said it was only a matter of time.

The sleeping lion woke on June 23, 1990, in Naples, Italy. Cameroon was pitted against Colombia, led by Carlos Valderrama, he of the famous shaggy blond perm and deceptive passing skills.

The first ninety scoreless minutes, Joey chewed on a frozen wet towel. In extra time, he squeezed his head between two couch pillows with his gold pendant clenched between his teeth. Shortly into the second overtime, Roger Milla made a calm little give-and-go with his left midfielder. Suddenly, Milla let the return go through, cut left, and eluded a slide tackle to break into the box. He slashed one past the keeper with his left foot.

It was the biggest goal in African history, but Milla celebrated like always — by dancing his jig with the corner flag. Joey celebrated by running down to Irving Street to wave his Cameroonian flag. By the time he got back, Milla had already struck again. Colombia's goalkeeper, René Higuita, liked to roam up the field behind his defenders. When Higuita failed to control a back-pass, Milla pounced, winning the ball with an open net in front of him.

Amazingly, because of his age, Roger Milla wasn't even supposed to be on the team. He was only named to the squad because Cameroon's president had ordered it, largely for sentimental reasons. But sometimes, sentimental reasons are the best reasons to do things.

It's been twenty years since that summer. I've never taken my boots off since. I've never gone a month without a match, and I've never again lacked for a reason to play.

Po Bronson
All-Time World Cup XI

Oliver Kahn
Marco Materazzi
Fabio Cannavaro
Leonardo
Lilian Thuram
Andrea Pirlo
Michael Ballack
Michel Platini
Diego Maradona
Ronaldo Nazario de Lima
Roger Milla

THE STORY OF THE CUPS

Frenchman Jules Rimet was the visionary behind the World Cup. The tournament's first trophy was named after him. Cast in gold plate, the cup was adorned with Nike, the Greek Goddess of Victory, her arms raised aloft in triumph. Every soccer player wanted to have his way with her.

During the Second World War, Italy possessed the trophy, having won the last prewar Finals in 1938. To prevent the Nazis stealing the Cup and marching it back to Hitler's sideboard, an Italian soccer official hid the prize in a shoe box underneath his bed. The Nazis looked in every stadium, soccer club, and under every Italian grandma's skirt but found nothing. Safe from the Nazis but not safe from common villainy.

The Jules Rimet Cup

England 1966, three months before the Finals kicked off. The Cup was on display in a church hall in London. Protecting the gold were some of England's finest security guards taking another tea break. The burglar struck with no fingerprint to be had. Scotland Yard was called to the task. Sherlocks combed England's underbelly looking for the golden chalice. The nation was embarrassed, the nitwit guards humiliated. A goldsmith was hired to forge a replica, in case the coppers failed to sniff out the thief.

Lucky for the Sherlocks, and FIFA, the day was saved by the snout of a trusted mongrel. Pickles was walking his master, when he noticed a package under the wheel of a car. From his master's voice came shock! He had found the stolen World Cup.

The trophy had been dumped by the burglar in a botched ransom swap but the crafty canine screwed things up by finding the swag first. Pickles quickly became a national hero, lauded by the winning England team, receiving the Dog of the Year Award, and given a year's supply of tinned food. Tragically, he met his end while chasing a cat up a tree. His leash wrapped around a branch, and Pickles swung from the gallows, like a criminal. It was a cruel irony.

In 1970, Brazil was handed the trophy to keep, having won the tournament for the third time. But in 1983, Brazilian security guards were on their tea break, and the Jules Rimet trophy was stolen again, never to be recovered. Scurrilous rumors abounded that secret agents from Argentina had pinched it for a cadre of ex-Nazis, still intent on fulfilling Hitler's twisted dreams. But the first World Cup was likely melted down for the gold. Someone is wearing it right now.

A new golden trophy was designed for the 1974 Finals in West Germany. "Kaiser" Franz Beckenbauer, the German captain, was the first player to get his hands on it. The baby is fourteen inches tall and weighs a sturdy fourteen pounds. A pair of safe hands is needed to cradle the prize. So don't give it to an Italian. They broke it. After Italy's win in the 2006 Final, a piece of the trophy's base fell off. After a search for some superglue, the errant piece was reattached, and the Italian team agreed not to kick it around anymore.

The present-day Cup

Didier Drogba, Ivory Coast

photo by Ryu Voelkel

THE WORLD CUP FINAL

★ ★ ★ ★ ★

ENGLAND VS. WEST GERMANY

Wembley Stadium, London, England
1966
Attendance: 98,000

Did the ball cross the goal line? That's the debate that rages to this day over one of the most historic Finals in history. With the game in extra time and tied at 2-2, England's Geoff Hurst smacked a shot that came down off the crossbar, and landed over the line if you were English, or on the line if you were German, or any other English haters. Fortunately, it was left to the referee and the linesman to decide. They took one look at the stoic English Queen sitting in the stands, and decided the image of their heads on pikes at Tower Bridge was something to avoid.

In the final seconds of the match, Hurst completed his hat trick with a fantastic strike, with fans already rushing the field. Match commentator Kenneth Wolstenholme etched his marvelous voice into sportscasting history with his memorable description of Hurst's final score: "There are fans on the field....They think it's all over.... It is now." England legend Bobby Moore lifted the trophy, and the Queen of England was happy with her knights.

Decades later, rumors surfaced that the tournament had been fixed. Former FIFA president, the elderly João Havelange, suggested that Brazil had been bashed out of the Finals due to English and German officials unfairly refereeing their games. Some old men have trouble with incontinence of the mouth. It was England's year. The players, Charlton, Stiles, Banks and Peters, became names engraved in English soccer folklore. Rule Britannia!

**WEST GERMANY
vs. HOLLAND**

Olimpiastadion,
Munich,
West Germany
1974
Attendance:
75,200

They were Dutch masters. They brought to the Final a new art form, Total Football. Each player could play any position in the team. They stroked the ball around the field like Van Gogh stroked his brush across the tulips. Open, free, and joyous to watch, the soccer world was high on Amsterdam. And the Dutch were playing against the Germans in the Final. Who would rule the world? The earth bit its nails as the 10th Final kicked off.

Right away, the Clockwork Orange Dutch spread the ball, flowing gracefully over the pitch, and suddenly there was Johan Cruyff bursting like a comet into Germany's inner lair. The Flying Dutchman had his legs machine-gunned out from under him. Penalty. 1-0. And the Germans had yet to touch the ball.

The Germans haircuts matched the Dutch for flair, but their uniforms had an oppositional feel, a stark black and white that suggested a lack of humor. Few found it funny when German striker Bernd Hölzenbein impersonated a submarine and dived inside the penalty box. The English referee was impressed, and awarded him a spot kick, instead of an Oscar. The only German with an Afro, Paul Breitner, torpedoed the penalty into the net, tying the score.

German engineering took over in the second half, and the Dutch tulip began to wilt, allowing Der Bomber to strike. Gerd Müller, the German ace striker, delivered the trophy to a thankful West German nation, still reeling from the calamity of terrorism that had ruined the 1972 Olympics when Israeli athletes were massacred. Der Kaiser Franz Beckenbauer,

The Dutch Master brought artistry to the game but not victory.

the German captain, lifted the new World Cup trophy, Brazil having kept the old one in 1970, as reward for winning the championship thrice. The golden cup stood out against the dark and gloomy sky. West Germany ruled the world.

The #10 on a soccer uniform is special. The greats Pelé and Maradona wore it. And in the 1998 World Cup Final, another legend was born wearing the #10, Zinedine "Zizou" Zidane. He carried France to victory over Brazil in a 3-0 triumph. The country was saved from its fin de siecle malaise. Millions poured onto the streets of Paris for the biggest party since Hitler got the red card in 1944. Zidane, the son of Algerian immigrants, was the new face of France.

FRANCE vs. BRAZIL
Stade de France,
Saint Denis,
France 1998
Attendance: 80,000

Pre-match controversy centered round Brazil's great hope, the striker Ronaldo. The South Americans held up the start of the match, Ronaldo's stomach seemingly stricken. Mocking fans suggested the bloat was due to an undigested pre-match chocolate croissant. While the world waited for the kickoff, Ronaldo hit the Pepto-Bismol, until he passed gas, no doubt with skill. The French, famous for their wines, cheese and low heart attack rates, remained calm and resisted the Brazilian mind games. When the teams finally emerged onto the field, the Brazilians were holding hands, like preschoolers out for a stroll. France was about to teach them a lesson. Zidane's two powerful headers and Petit's goal in the dying seconds of the game sent France into paradise. World champions for the first time, two days before Bastille Day, "La Marseillaise" was never sung louder. Zidane's image was projected onto L'Arc de Triomphe with a simple message emblazoned across Napoleonic France's greatest landmark—*Merci Zizou.*

Penalty kicks are like home runs, the one-shot moment. In the 1994 Final, they decided the winner of the World Cup Final. It was ugly, like many of the hairstyles that year. Vice President Al Gore, before he invented the Internet and melting planets, handed over the trophy to the unfortunately named Brazilian captain, Dunga. After the Final, there was a smell of fertilizer in the smog-choked Southern California air. The roots of Major League Soccer were about to pop up. Finally, at glacial speed, America had arrived as a presence on Planet Soccer.

Taking a penalty in the World Cup Final can shoot a man down. His manhood is questioned. Does he have the nerve to slot home from twelve yards? It looks easy. It never is. And Roberto Baggio, the Italian ace, will long be remembered for his blown effort that handed the trophy to Brazil. His disastrous kick was high enough to be a field goal in the other football. The Brazilians danced around him, and another tragic Italian opera was over.

Post Finals, debate raged across the soccer universe. Should penalty kicks decide the outcome of the biggest game of all? Some suggested a replay, and tossing a coin was flipped as an idea but the heads at FIFA decided the agony of the penalty spot was to remain the chosen decider. Inevitably, there would be more Baggios.

The missed penalty shot ended the tragic Italian opera.

FRANCE vs. ITALY

Olimpiastadion,
Berlin, Germany
2006
Attendance:
69,000

The antagonists in the 2006 Final were old enemies, the main actors fighting over honor, the foreshadowing of missed chances, the image of rejection reflecting off the gold of the World Cup itself. It was theater, darlings!

Few remember the game; everyone remembers the head butt. Most reasonable people understood Zidane's attack on the thuggish Italian defender Materazzi. Hearing that his sister was a whore from a man who had kicked him for ninety minutes was too much for the street-fighting Zizou. But before the famous clout, Zidane had used his head in proper fashion to prompt the save of the tournament from the Italian goalie, Buffon.

Seven hundred fifty million people around the world watched Zidane being sent off, walking past the dazzling World Cup trophy, disappearing into the darkness of the tunnel. He would never play again. Zidane had no regrets. Honor before death. The French *coq sportif* crowed in admiration for their retired hero. But France went down in penaltics, the second Final to be decided from twelve yards.

Deservedly, Fabio Cannavaro, the Italian defender and captain, lifted the trophy. His superb defending qualities were worthy of his award as player of the tournament. Italy nabbed another cup for the sideboard, their fourth, and went home to their mothers and sisters, champions again.

Front and back cover:

Photo of soccer ball by Ian McKinnell/Photographer's Choice/Getty Images

Front cover:

Photo of World Cup © Christian Liewig/TempSports/Corbis

Photo of man with sign by Nikolaus Ostermann

Photo of two players courtesy of AFP/Getty Images

Photo of fans by Altrendo Images/Altrendo/Getty Images

Back cover:

Photo of player kicking soccer ball by Comstock Images/Jupiter Images Unlimited

Photo of fan by Sandy Bailey/Getty Images

Photo of stadium by Richard Ross/The Image Bank/Getty Images

ACKNOWLEDGMENTS

We would like to thank Danielle Svetcov, a great agent who actually gives a shit. Kim Gledhill, Art Director, has been a revelation. She is an amazing artist and a joy to work with; this book would not have happened without her. Thanks to Mark Chait and all the Penguins. Emma Cortese and Julie Brown researched their asses off. A big *Merci!* to Malik—an African soccer player in New York—for reenacting Pienaar's flip. MaryAnn Miller took two truly huge road trips and some excellent photos. Liu Yuhua is a fantastic artist and an amazing caricaturist. A shout-out to photographers: Michael E. Kane, W. Jarrett Campbell, Stefan Meisel, and Ryu Voelkel. *Gracias* to Maricarmen and Beth, and much appreciation to David Sillen for all his help and to Thomas for his willingness to kick in. And a great thanks to the Snow Leopard, Arielle Eckstut, a constant source of inspiration and illumination, and a person of seemingly limitless patience when it comes to sitting through yet another soccer game. Big shout from the terraces for Ana, Angela and Grant for allowing the play to continue. And to Johnny Miller and Frank McGuire.

CONTRIBUTING WRITERS

Irvine Welsh is the bestselling author of *Trainspotting* and seven other novels. He supports Hibs.

Po Bronson is the bestselling author of *What Should I Do With My Life?*, *Why Do I Love These People?*, and *NurtureShock, New Thinking About Children* (with Ashley Merryman).

Simon Kuper is the soccer correspondent for the *Financial Times*, and has written for many publications. His latest book is *Soccernomics: Why England Loses, Why Germany and Brazil Win, and Why the U.S., Japan, Australia, Turkey—and Even Iraq—Are Destined to Become the Kings of the World's Most Popular Sport* (with Stefan Szymanski).

Alan Black is the author of the memoir *Kick the Balls—An Offensive Suburban Odyssey*. www.alanblack.info

David Henry Sterry is the author of 11 books, a former hardman, and a soccer fanatic who takes no prisoners. www.davidhenrysterry.com

Kim Sillen Gledhill is the graphic designer and illustrator of this book. All of the internal graphics, drawings, photo-retouching, and toy soccer player imagery are her work (with the exception of the villain drawing, etchings and Liu Yuhua's caricatures). www.kimgledhill.com

Liu Yuhua drew the charcoal caricatures as noted.

Photographers:

W. Jarrett Campbell / Triangle Soccer Fanatics: pages 28 and 37 www.TriSoccerFan.com

Ryu Voelkel: pages 16, 51, 58, 73, 81, 91, 97, 103, 112-113 and 128 www.ryusha.com www.flickr.com/photos/ryusha/

Michael E. Kane: pages 38, 39, 40, 41 and 43 cadmanvta@pacbell.net

David Henry Sterry: Fan photos, pages 33-35, 66, 74, 98 and 127

Stefan Meisel: pages 2, 12, 13 and 64 www.flickr.com/stefanmeisel/ Stefan Meisel is a German photographer who lives in Abidjan, in the Ivory Coast, West Africa. His photos of African life and soccer are published in many Ivorian and German newspapers, as well as several worldwide magazines and publications.